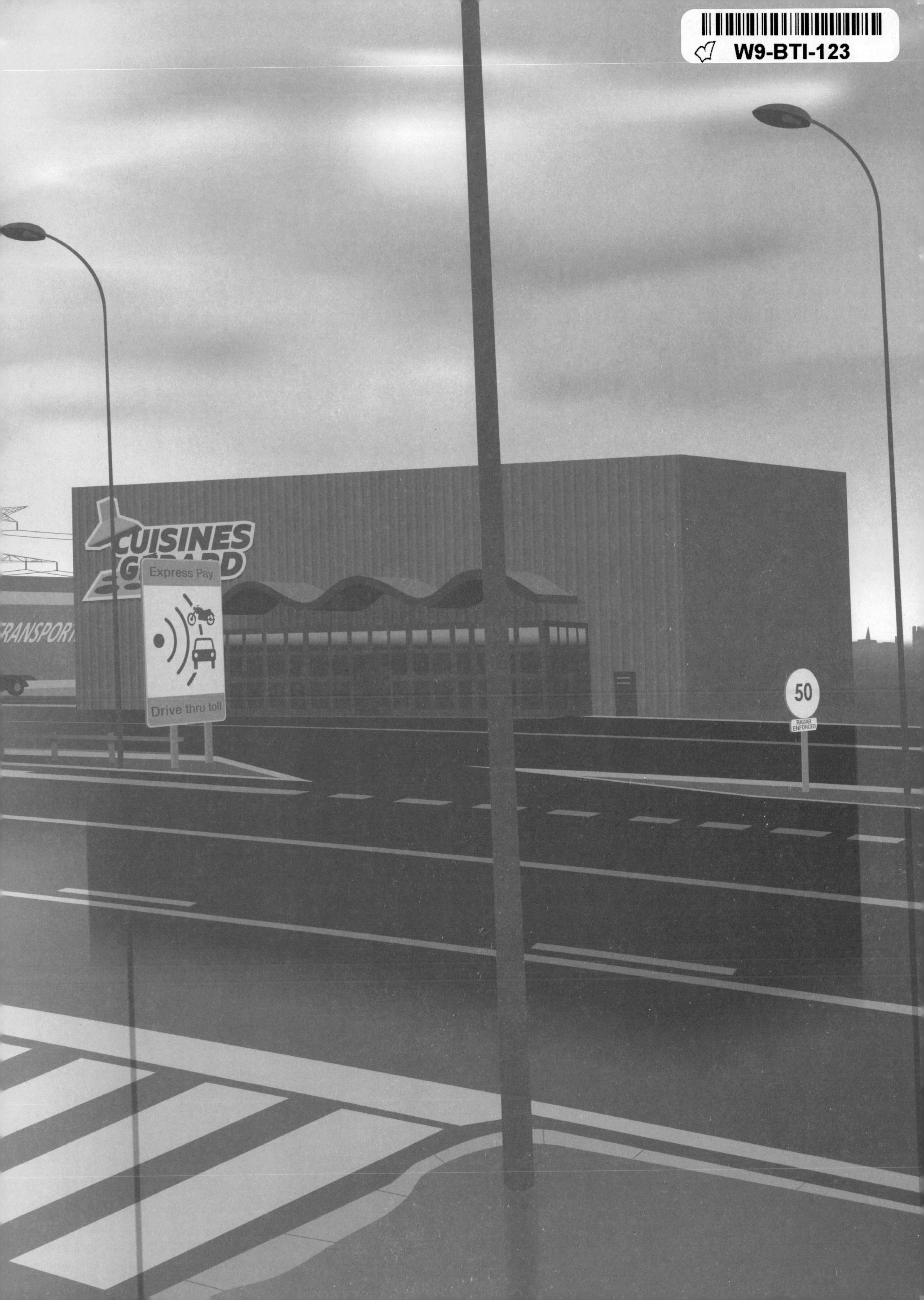
CUISINES
Express Pay
Drive thru toll
50
RADAR ENFORCED

ARTHUR DE PINS

Zombillenium

1. Gretchen

NANTIER • BEALL • MINOUSTCHINE
Publishing inc.
new york

Also available:
Zombillenium, vol. 2, $14.99
And other spoofs of horror and fantasy:
Boneyard, vols. 1-7
The Dungeon series (multiple volumes)

SEE MORE AT NBMPUB.COM
AND ZOMBILLENIUM.COM

We have over 200 titles available
NBM
160 Broadway, Suite 700, East Wing
New York, NY 10038
Catalog available by request
If ordering by mail add $4 P&H 1st item, $1 each addt'l

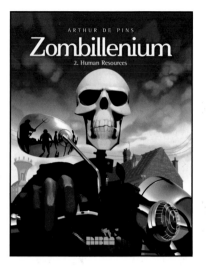

I wish to thank Frédéric Niffle for having proposed
one day, that I tell a story about monsters.

Any resemblance between the Gretchen character and
Aurelie C. is unintended only to the extent that Gretchen
begins lacing her shoes with the left foot.

ARTHUR DE PINS

ISBN 978-1-56163-734-8
© Dupuis, 2010
Library of Congress Control Number: 2013936651

Printed in China
1st published August 2013
2nd printing June 2014

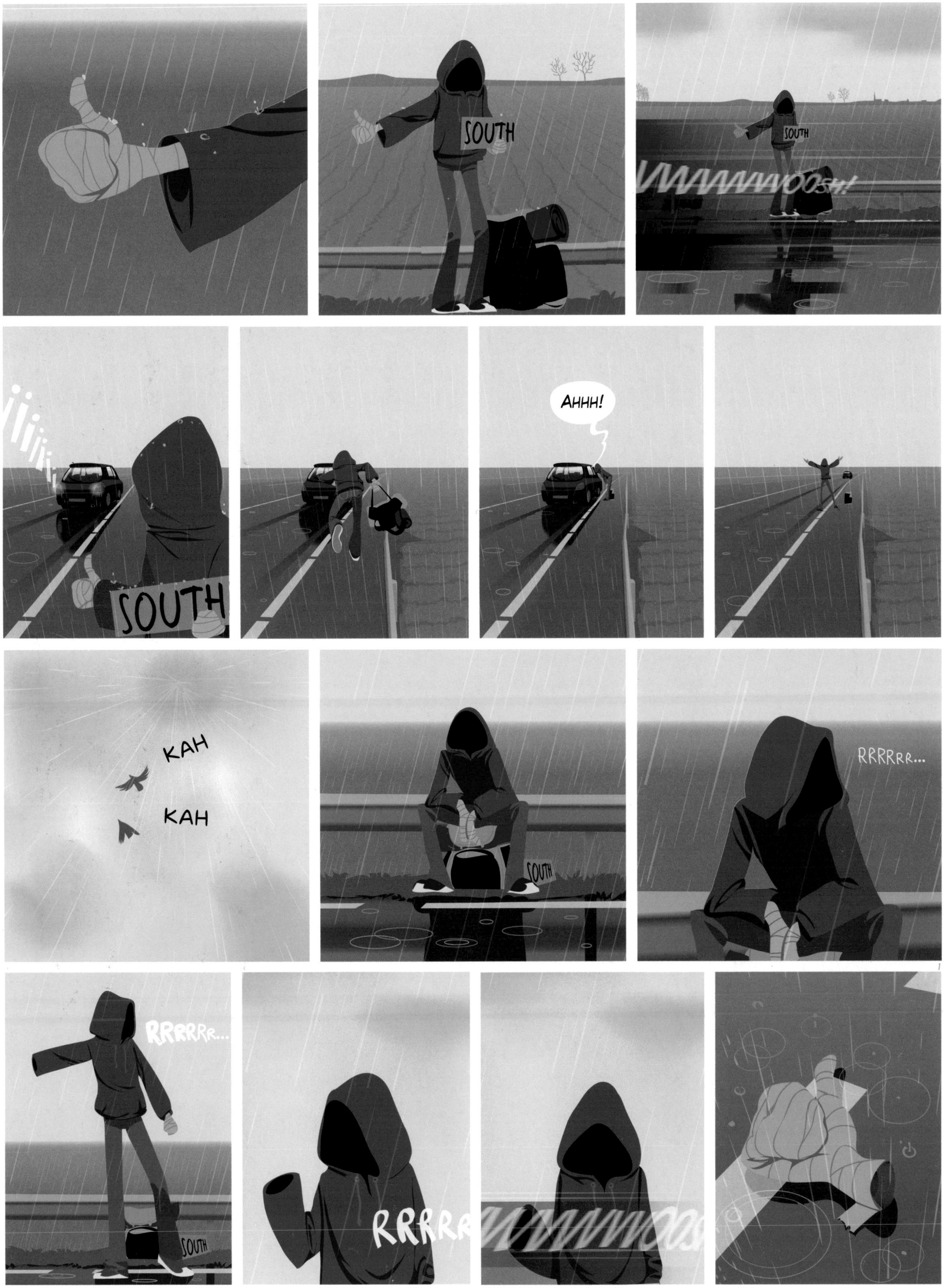
SOUTH
SOUTH
VVVVVVVVOOSH!
SOUTH
AHHH!
KAH
KAH
SOUTH
RRRRRRR...
RRRRRr...
SOUTH
RRRRR

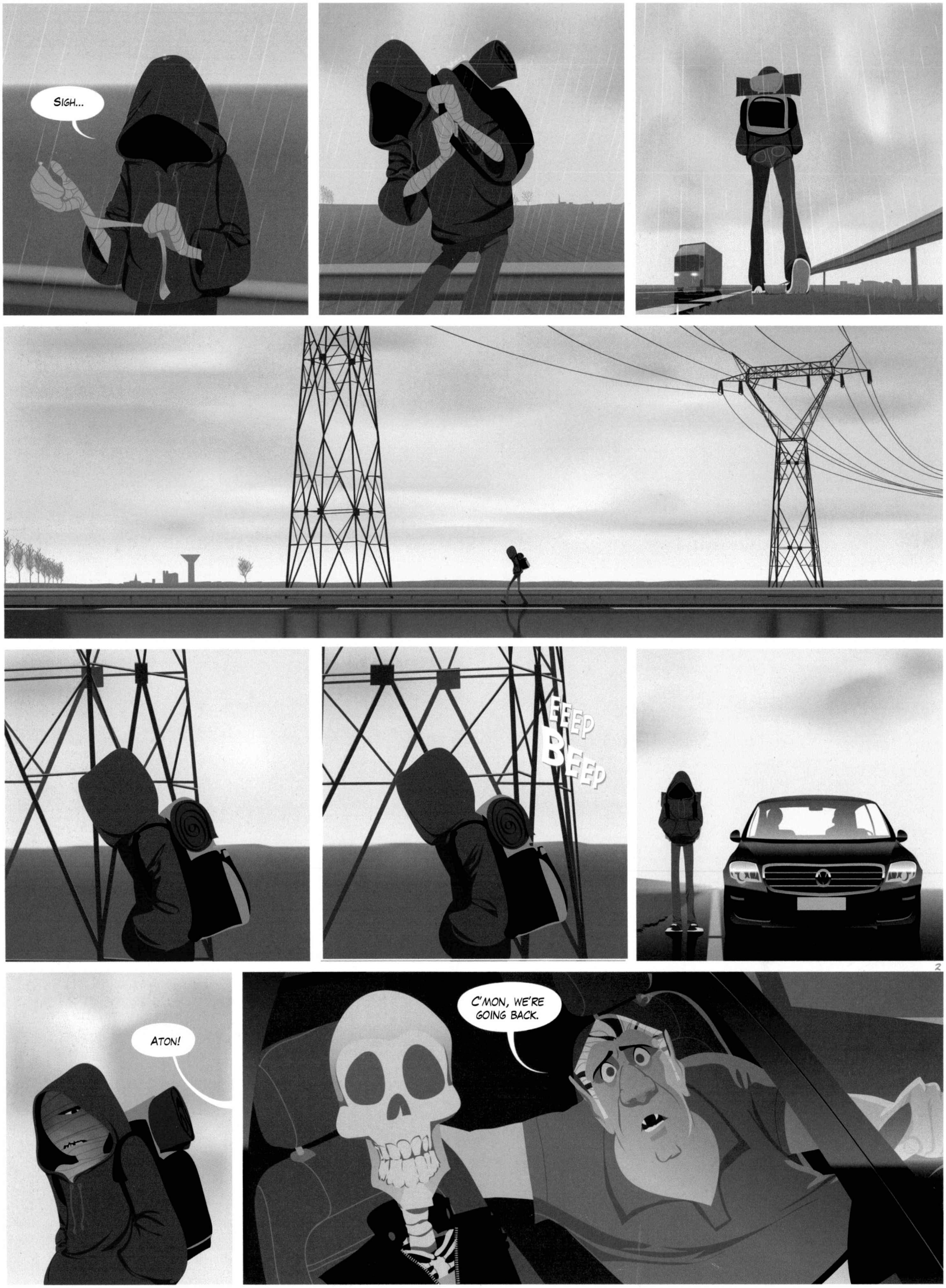
SIGH...
BEEEP BEEEP
ATON!
C'MON, WE'RE GOING BACK.

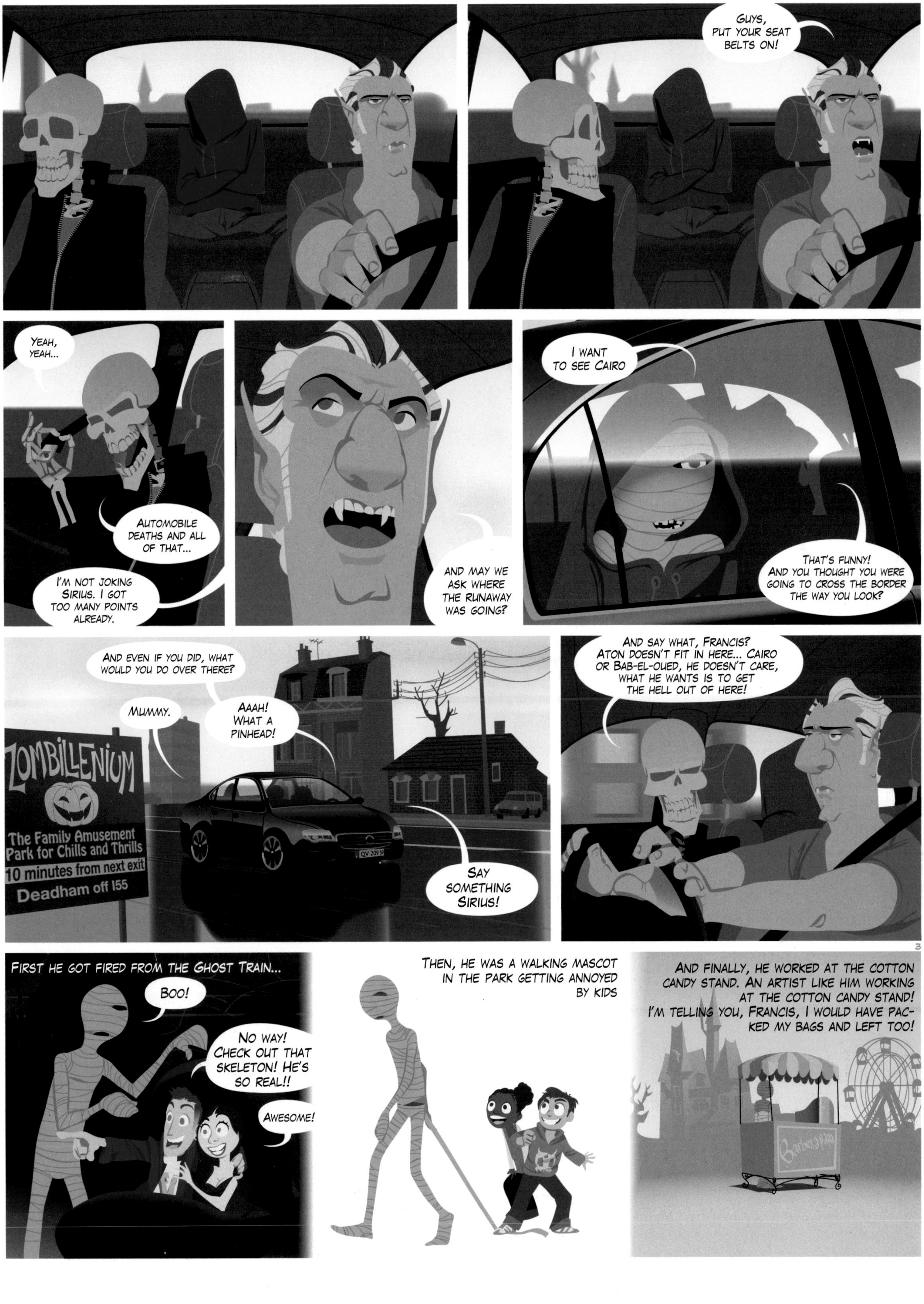
GUYS, PUT YOUR SEAT BELTS ON!
YEAH, YEAH...
AUTOMOBILE DEATHS AND ALL OF THAT...
I'M NOT JOKING SIRIUS. I GOT TOO MANY POINTS ALREADY.
AND MAY WE ASK WHERE THE RUNAWAY WAS GOING?
I WANT TO SEE CAIRO
THAT'S FUNNY! AND YOU THOUGHT YOU WERE GOING TO CROSS THE BORDER THE WAY YOU LOOK?
AND EVEN IF YOU DID, WHAT WOULD YOU DO OVER THERE?
MUMMY.
AAAH! WHAT A PINHEAD!
ZOMBILLENIUM
The Family Amusement Park for Chills and Thrills
10 minutes from next exit
Deadham off I55
SAY SOMETHING SIRIUS!
AND SAY WHAT, FRANCIS? ATON DOESN'T FIT IN HERE... CAIRO OR BAB-EL-OUED, HE DOESN'T CARE, WHAT HE WANTS IS TO GET THE HELL OUT OF HERE!
FIRST HE GOT FIRED FROM THE GHOST TRAIN...
BOO!
NO WAY! CHECK OUT THAT SKELETON! HE'S SO REAL!!
AWESOME!
THEN, HE WAS A WALKING MASCOT IN THE PARK GETTING ANNOYED BY KIDS
AND FINALLY, HE WORKED AT THE COTTON CANDY STAND. AN ARTIST LIKE HIM WORKING AT THE COTTON CANDY STAND! I'M TELLING YOU, FRANCIS, I WOULD HAVE PACKED MY BAGS AND LEFT TOO!

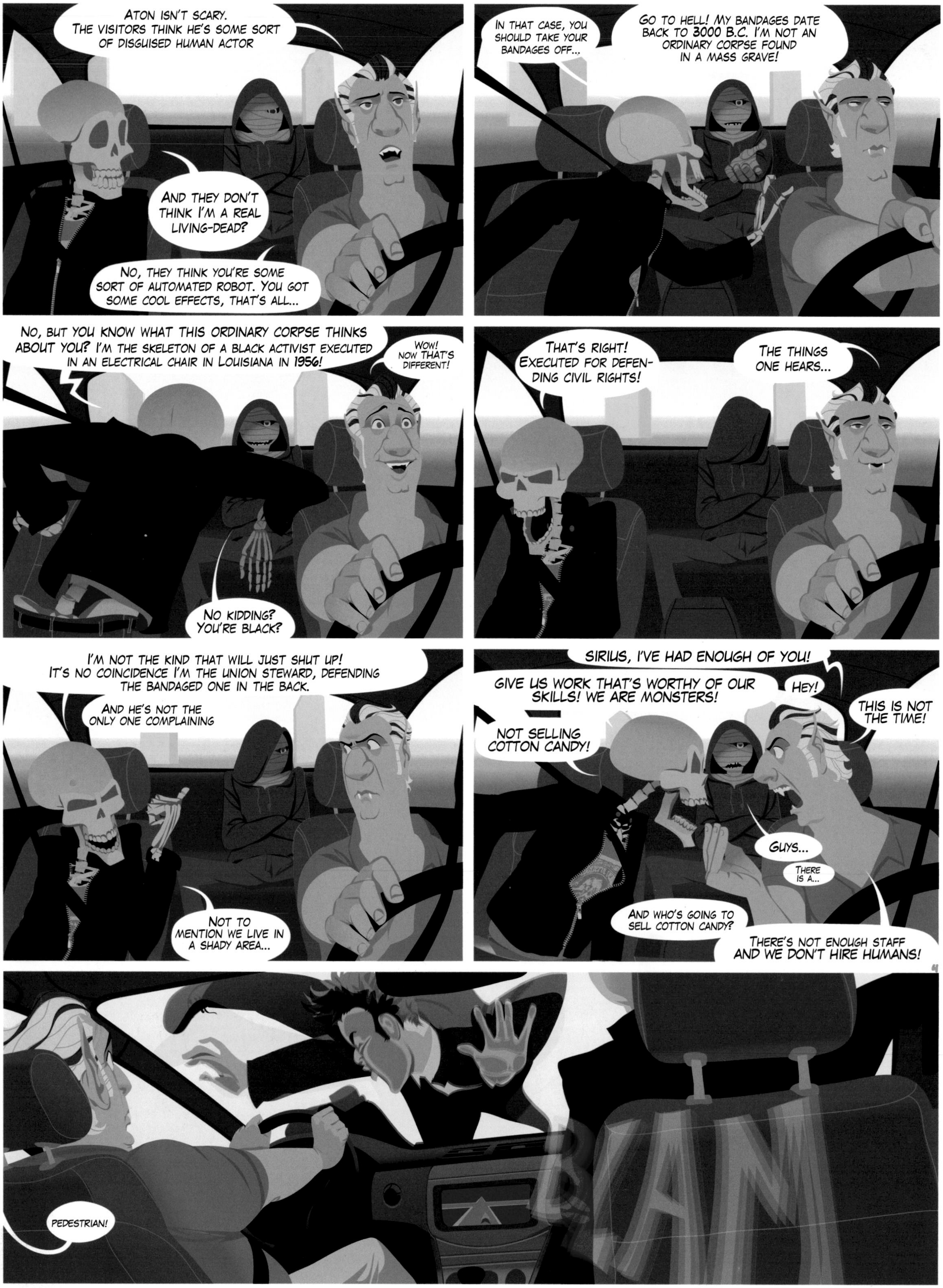

Aton isn't scary. The visitors think he's some sort of disguised human actor
And they don't think I'm a real living-dead?
No, they think you're some sort of automated robot. You got some cool effects, that's all...
In that case, you should take your bandages off...
Go to hell! My bandages date back to 3000 B.C. I'm not an ordinary corpse found in a mass grave!
No, but you know what this ordinary corpse thinks about you? I'm the skeleton of a black activist executed in an electrical chair in Louisiana in 1956!
Wow! Now that's different!
No kidding? You're black?
That's right! Executed for defending civil rights!
The things one hears...
I'm not the kind that will just shut up! It's no coincidence I'm the union steward, defending the bandaged one in the back.
And he's not the only one complaining
Not to mention we live in a shady area...
Sirius, I've had enough of you!
Give us work that's worthy of our skills! We are monsters!
Hey!
This is not the time!
Not selling cotton candy!
Guys...
There is a...
And who's going to sell cotton candy?
There's not enough staff and we don't hire humans!
Pedestrian!

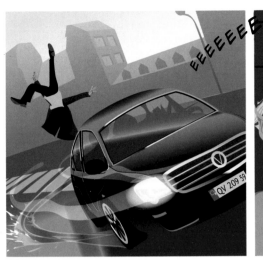
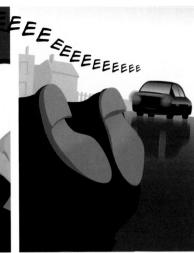
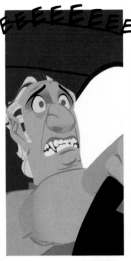
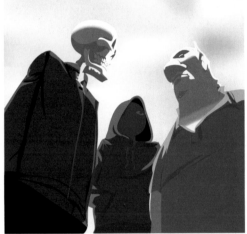
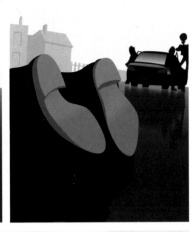

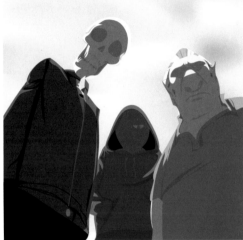
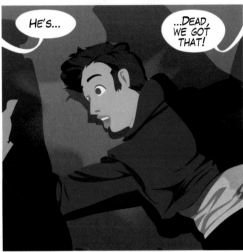
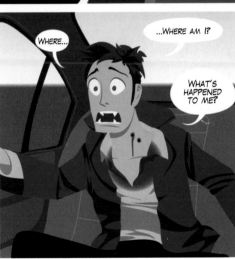

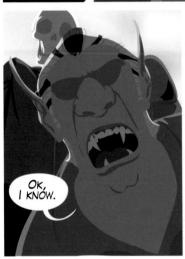
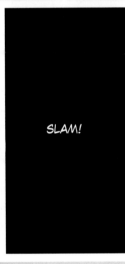
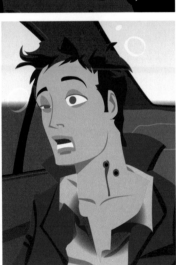

5

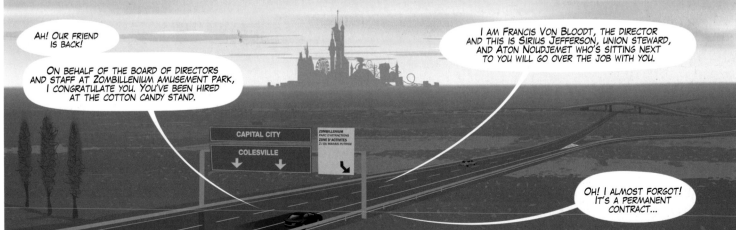

HALLOWEEN, SURE. 'NUTHER WAY TO SPEND YOUR MONEY, BUT OK.

I CAN GO FOR THAT.

THE KIDS LIKE IT.

BUT THEIR DAMN NUT JOB AMUSEMENT PARK,

NO WAY!

YO, JOE! NO NEED TO YELL!

YOU KNOW WHAT USED TO BE THERE? EH? A CEMETERY! THAT'S WHAT!

I CALL THAT SACRILEGE!

IT'S DISRESPECTFUL THEM MAKIN' MONEY ON TOP OF THIS!

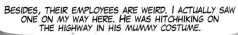

BESIDES, THEIR EMPLOYEES ARE WEIRD. I ACTUALLY SAW ONE ON MY WAY HERE. HE WAS HITCHHIKING ON THE HIGHWAY IN HIS MUMMY COSTUME.

WHAT IF YOU JUST BOUGHT ME A DRINK INSTEAD OF WHINING!

EH?

WANNA DRINK MISS?

SHIRLEY TEMPLE.

C'MON, AL, GET HER A GLASS OF WINE OR SUMTHIN'

C'MON JOE, SHE MUST BE 14 YEARS OLD.

SO WHAT? SHE'S GOT BOOBS! THAT MAKES HER A WOMAN, RIGHT?

JOE, YOU'RE DRUNK, STOP IT!

I KNOW WHAT I'M SAYING!

C'MON, SIT DOWN HERE...

WHAT'S THAT YOU'RE WEARING? YOU DON'T HAPPEN TO WORK AT ZOMBI-THING, DO YOU?

SO TELL ME. YOUR BOYFRIEND IS A VAMPIRE, IS THAT IT?

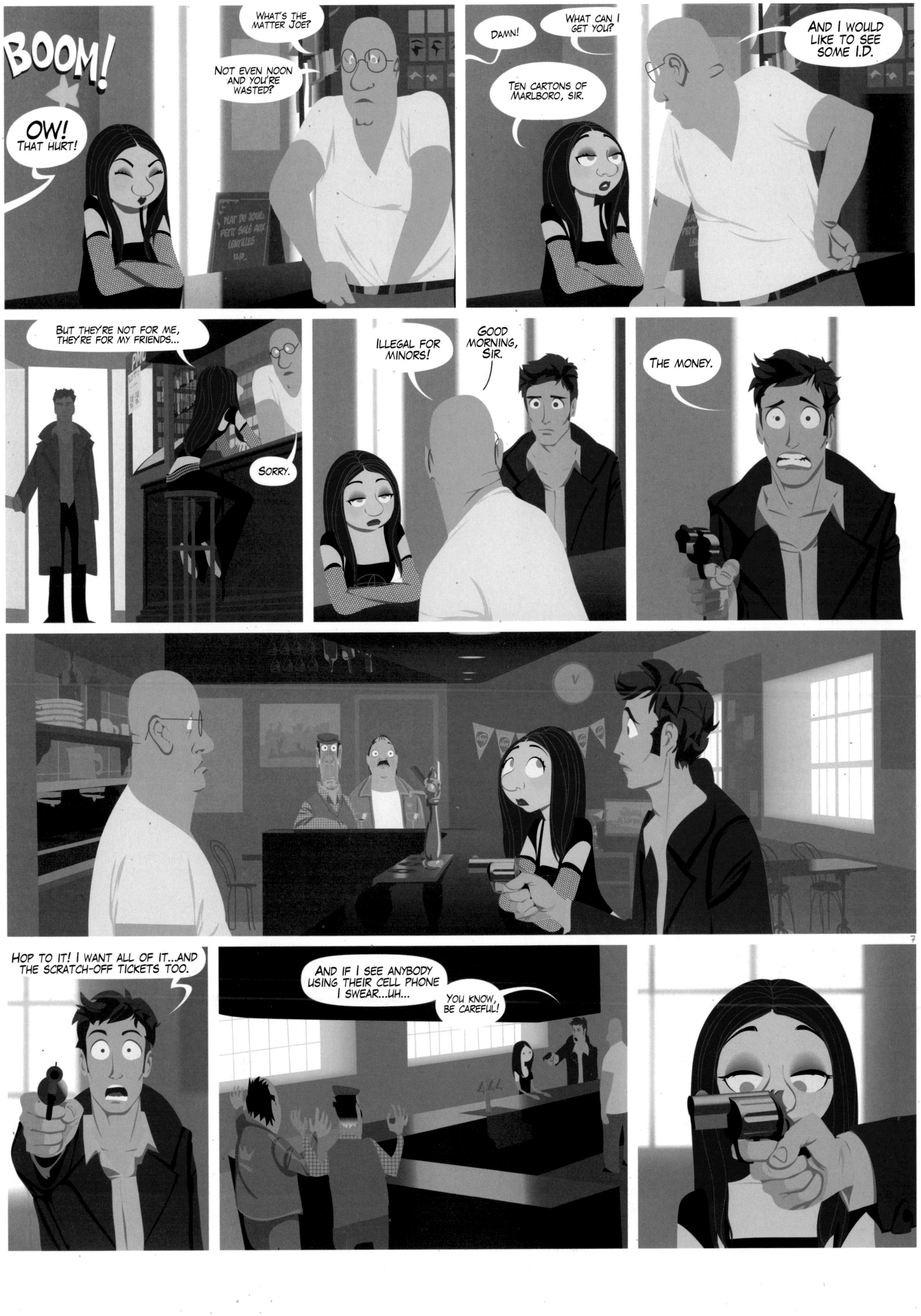
BOOM!
OW! THAT HURT!
WHAT'S THE MATTER JOE?
NOT EVEN NOON AND YOU'RE WASTED?
DAMN!
WHAT CAN I GET YOU?
TEN CARTONS OF MARLBORO, SIR.
AND I WOULD LIKE TO SEE SOME I.D.
BUT THEY'RE NOT FOR ME, THEY'RE FOR MY FRIENDS...
SORRY.
ILLEGAL FOR MINORS!
GOOD MORNING, SIR.
THE MONEY.
HOP TO IT! I WANT ALL OF IT...AND THE SCRATCH-OFF TICKETS TOO.
AND IF I SEE ANYBODY USING THEIR CELL PHONE I SWEAR...UH...
YOU KNOW, BE CAREFUL!

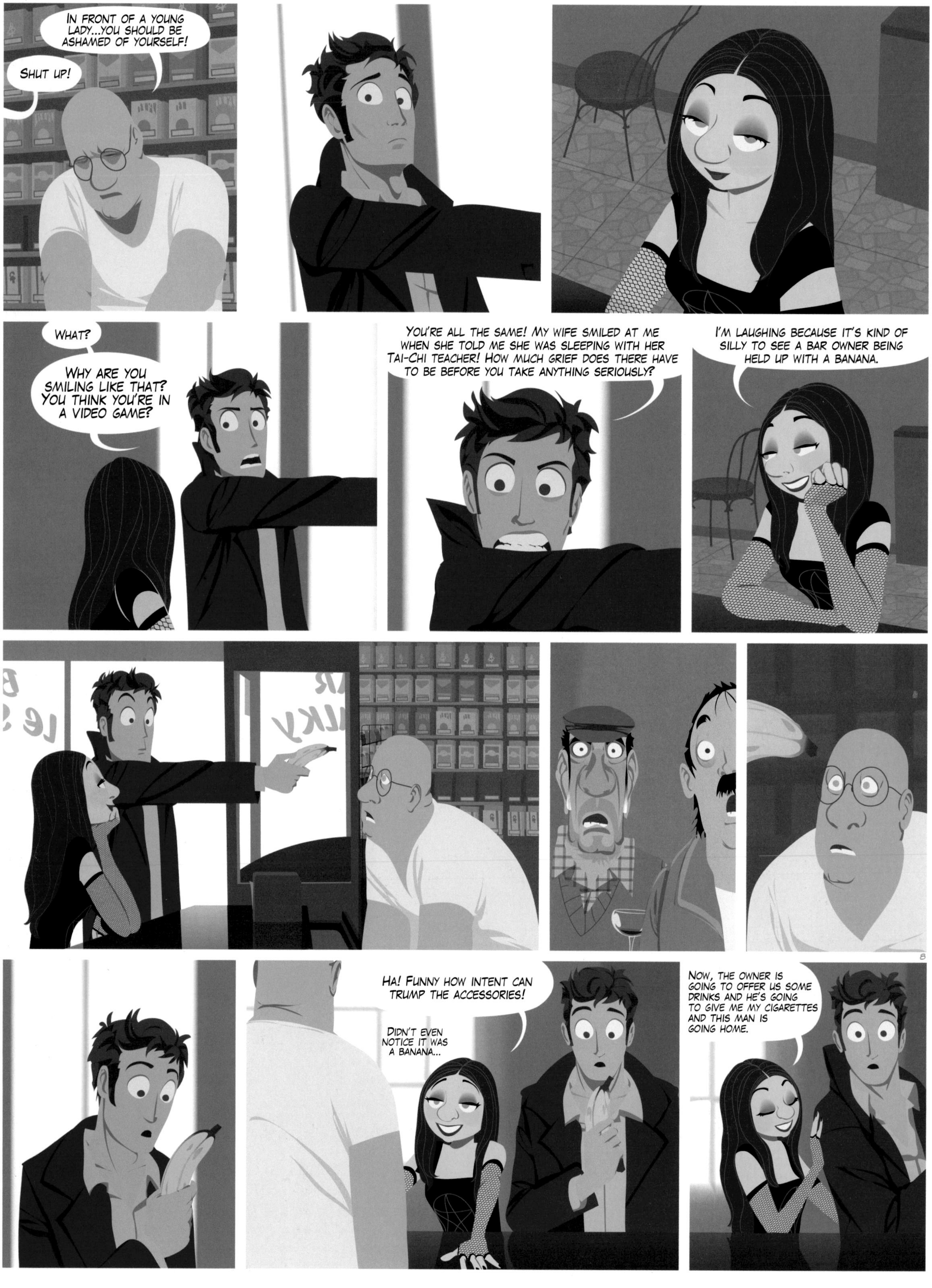

In front of a young lady...you should be ashamed of yourself!
Shut up!
What?
Why are you smiling like that? You think you're in a video game?
You're all the same! My wife smiled at me when she told me she was sleeping with her Tai-Chi teacher! How much grief does there have to be before you take anything seriously?
I'm laughing because it's kind of silly to see a bar owner being held up with a banana.
Ha! Funny how intent can trump the accessories!
Didn't even notice it was a banana...
Now, the owner is going to offer us some drinks and he's going to give me my cigarettes and this man is going home.

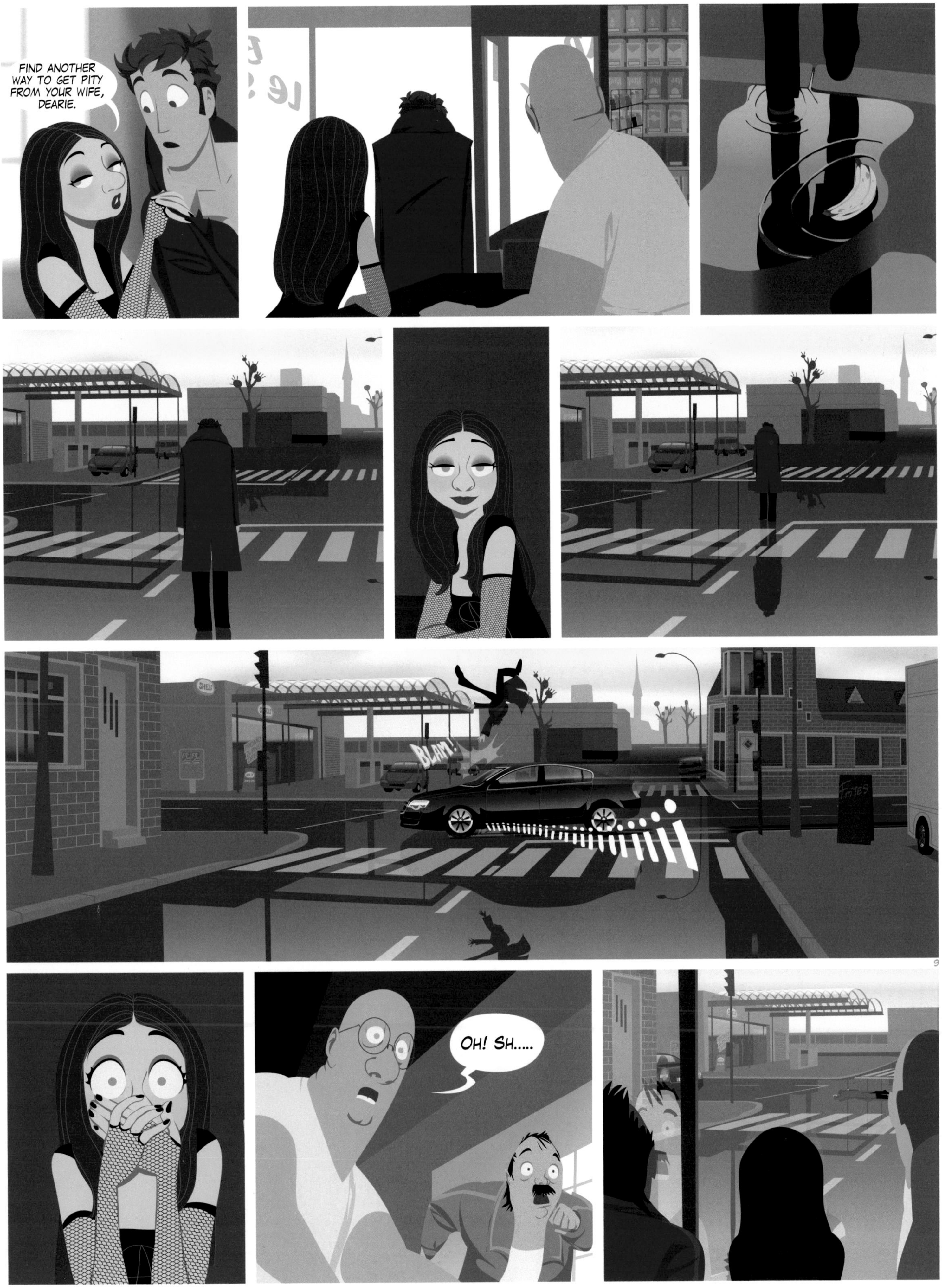
FIND ANOTHER WAY TO GET PITY FROM YOUR WIFE, DEARIE.
BLAM!
Frites
OH! SH.....

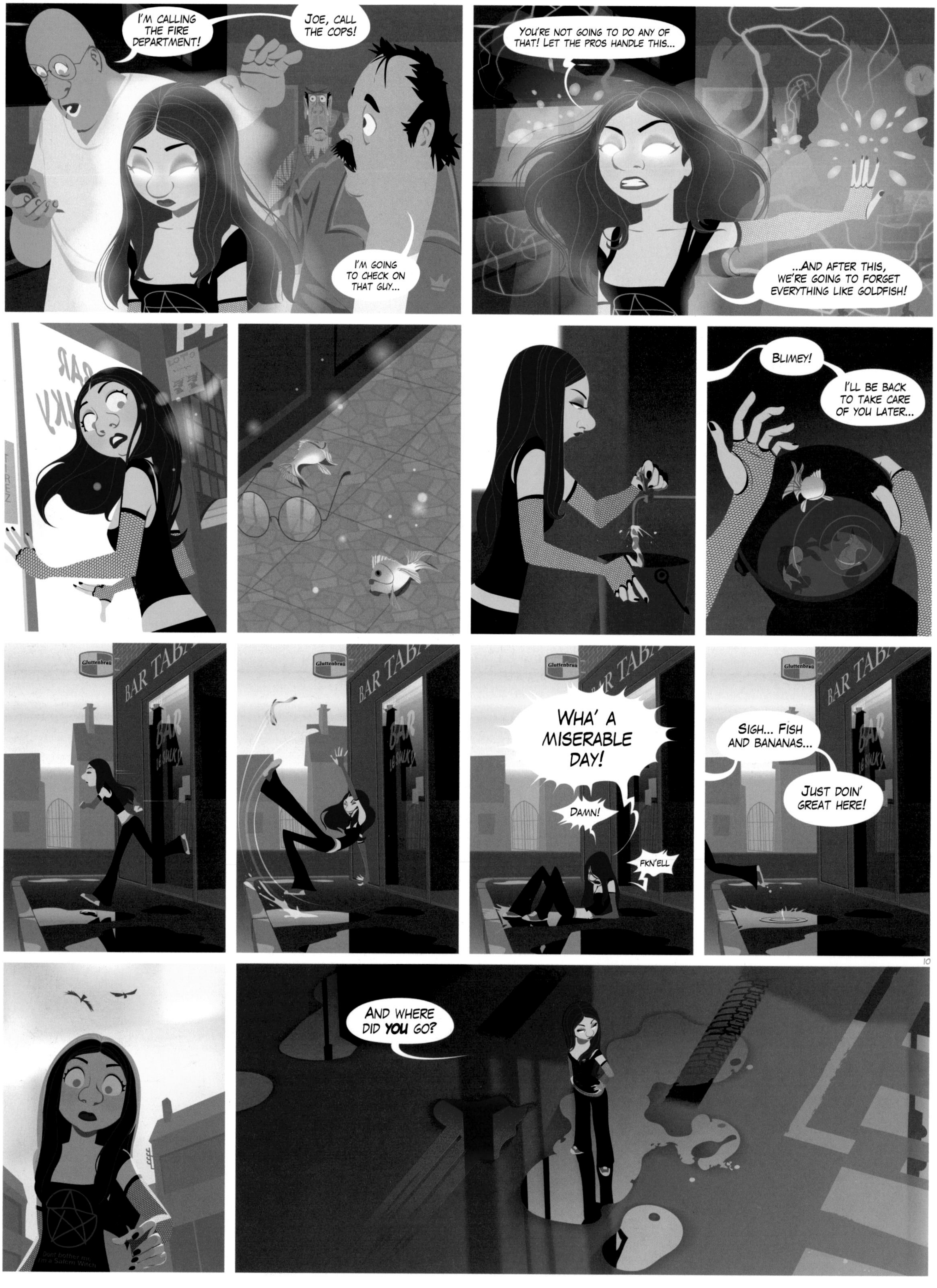
I'M CALLING THE FIRE DEPARTMENT!
JOE, CALL THE COPS!
I'M GOING TO CHECK ON THAT GUY...
YOU'RE NOT GOING TO DO ANY OF THAT! LET THE PROS HANDLE THIS...
...AND AFTER THIS, WE'RE GOING TO FORGET EVERYTHING LIKE GOLDFISH!
BLIMEY!
I'LL BE BACK TO TAKE CARE OF YOU LATER...
WHA' A MISERABLE DAY!
DAMN!
FKN'ELL
SIGH... FISH AND BANANAS...
JUST DOIN' GREAT HERE!
AND WHERE DID YOU GO?

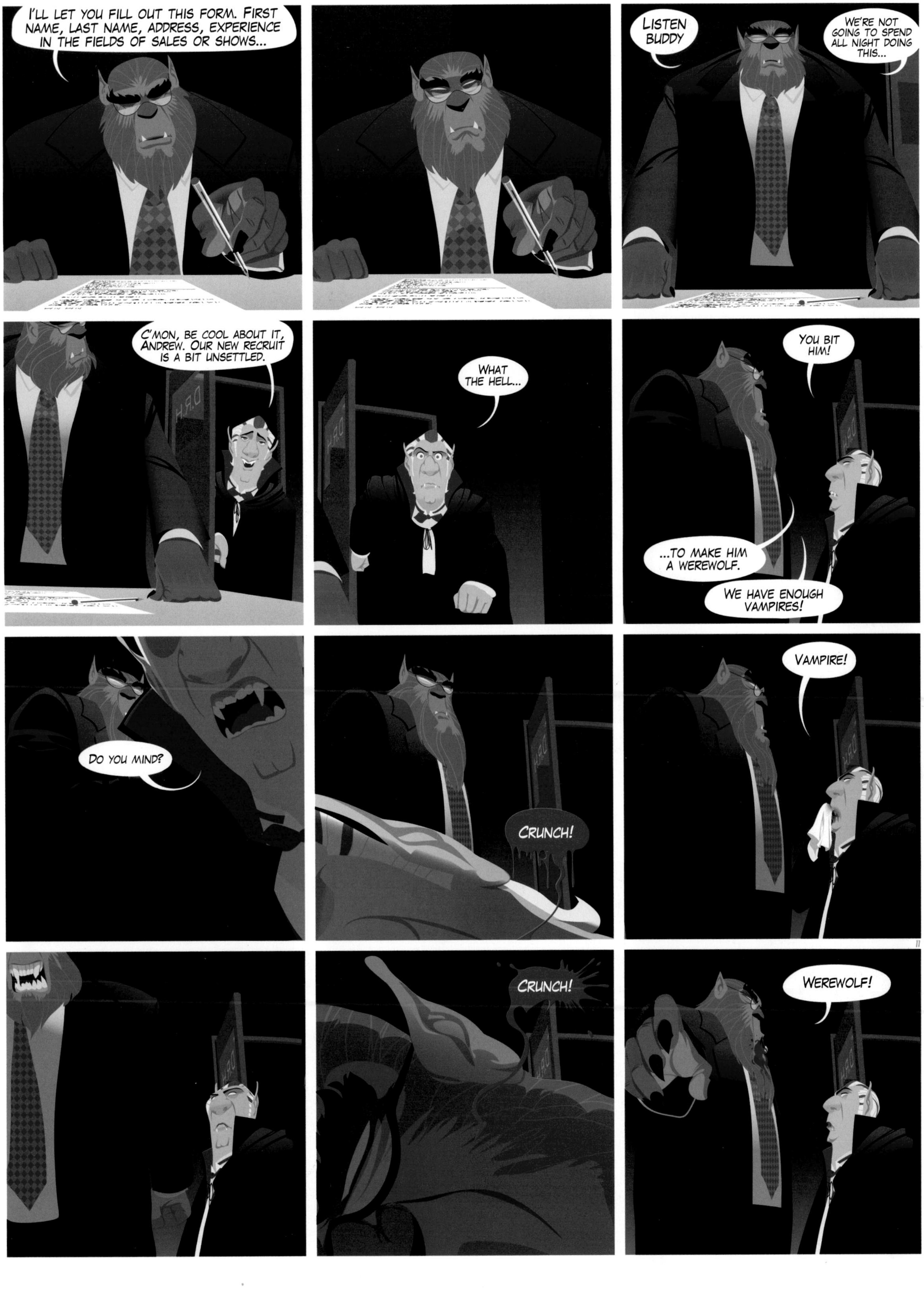
I'LL LET YOU FILL OUT THIS FORM. FIRST NAME, LAST NAME, ADDRESS, EXPERIENCE IN THE FIELDS OF SALES OR SHOWS...
LISTEN BUDDY
WE'RE NOT GOING TO SPEND ALL NIGHT DOING THIS...
C'MON, BE COOL ABOUT IT, ANDREW. OUR NEW RECRUIT IS A BIT UNSETTLED.
WHAT THE HELL...
YOU BIT HIM!
...TO MAKE HIM A WEREWOLF.
WE HAVE ENOUGH VAMPIRES!
DO YOU MIND?
CRUNCH!
VAMPIRE!
CRUNCH!
WEREWOLF!

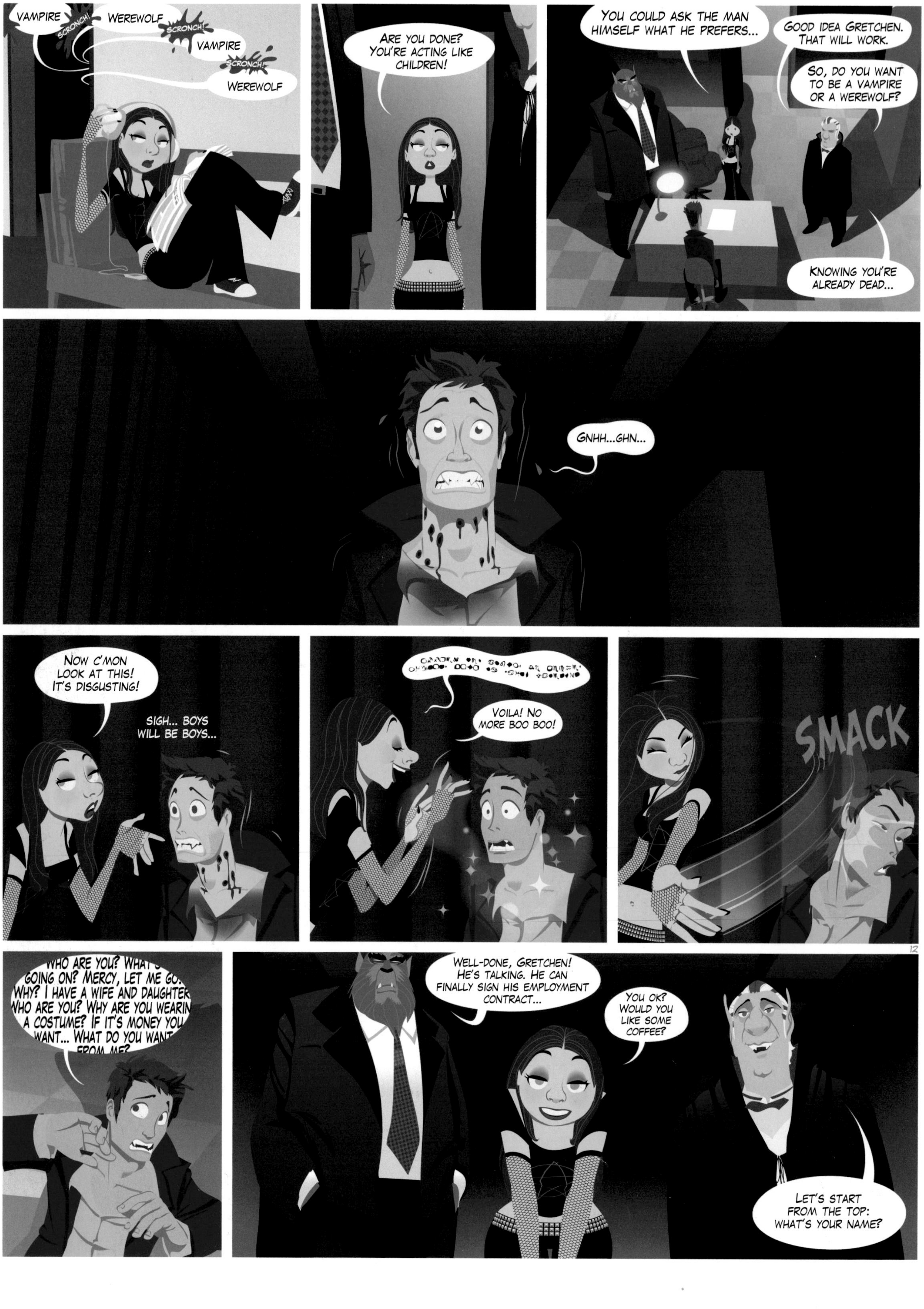
VAMPIRE
SCRONCH!
WEREWOLF
SCRONCH!
VAMPIRE
SCRONCH!
WEREWOLF
ARE YOU DONE? YOU'RE ACTING LIKE CHILDREN!
YOU COULD ASK THE MAN HIMSELF WHAT HE PREFERS...
GOOD IDEA GRETCHEN. THAT WILL WORK.
SO, DO YOU WANT TO BE A VAMPIRE OR A WEREWOLF?
KNOWING YOU'RE ALREADY DEAD...
GNHH...GHN...
NOW C'MON LOOK AT THIS! IT'S DISGUSTING!
SIGH... BOYS WILL BE BOYS...
VOILA! NO MORE BOO BOO!
SMACK
WHO ARE YOU? WHAT'S GOING ON? MERCY, LET ME GO! WHY? I HAVE A WIFE AND DAUGHTER. WHO ARE YOU? WHY ARE YOU WEARING A COSTUME? IF IT'S MONEY YOU WANT... WHAT DO YOU WANT FROM ME?
WELL-DONE, GRETCHEN! HE'S TALKING. HE CAN FINALLY SIGN HIS EMPLOYMENT CONTRACT...
YOU OK? WOULD YOU LIKE SOME COFFEE?
LET'S START FROM THE TOP: WHAT'S YOUR NAME?

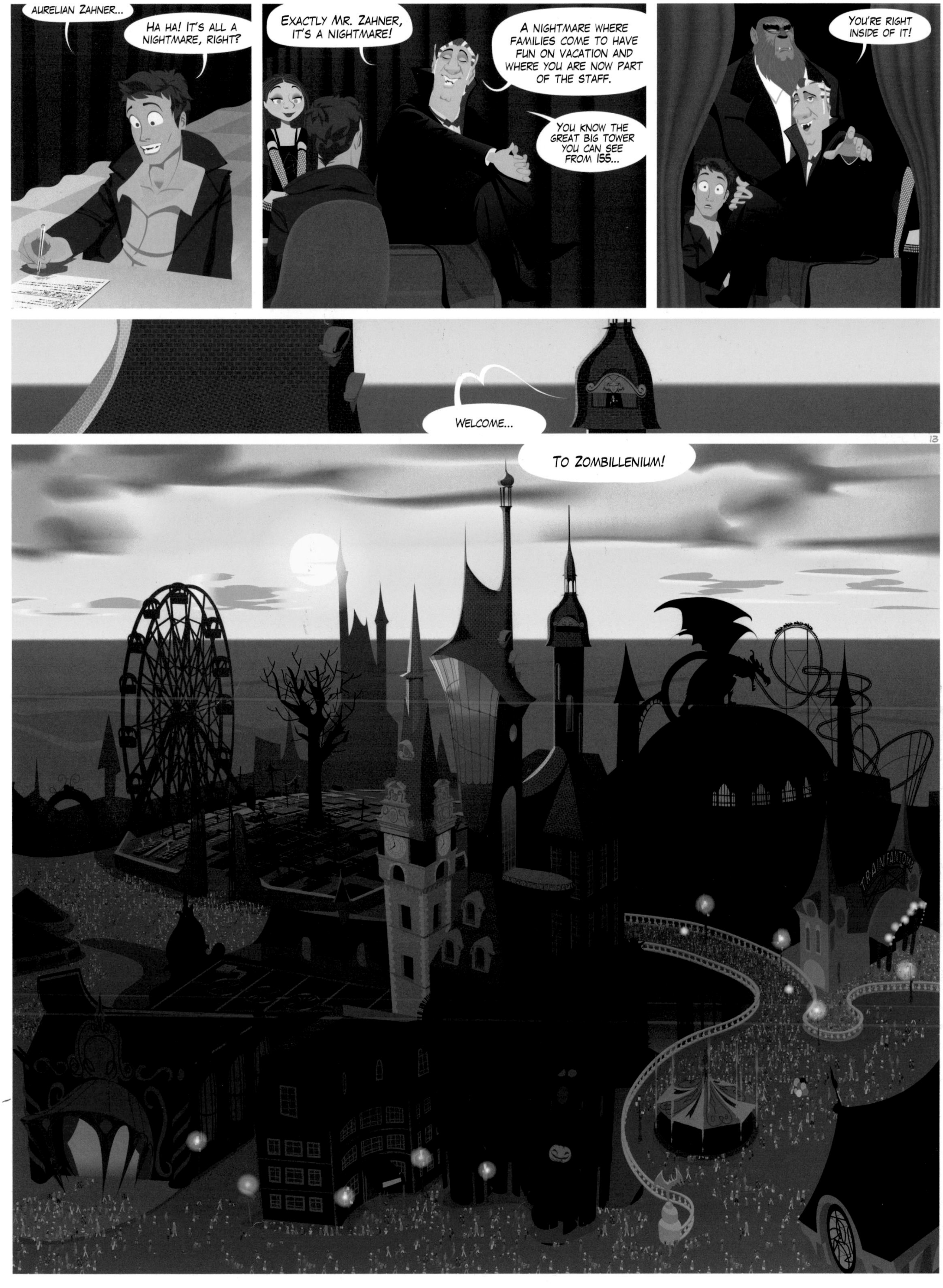
Aurelian Zahner...
Ha ha! It's all a nightmare, right?
Exactly Mr. Zahner, it's a nightmare!
A nightmare where families come to have fun on vacation and where you are now part of the staff.
You know the great big tower you can see from I55...
You're right inside of it!
Welcome...
To Zombillenium!

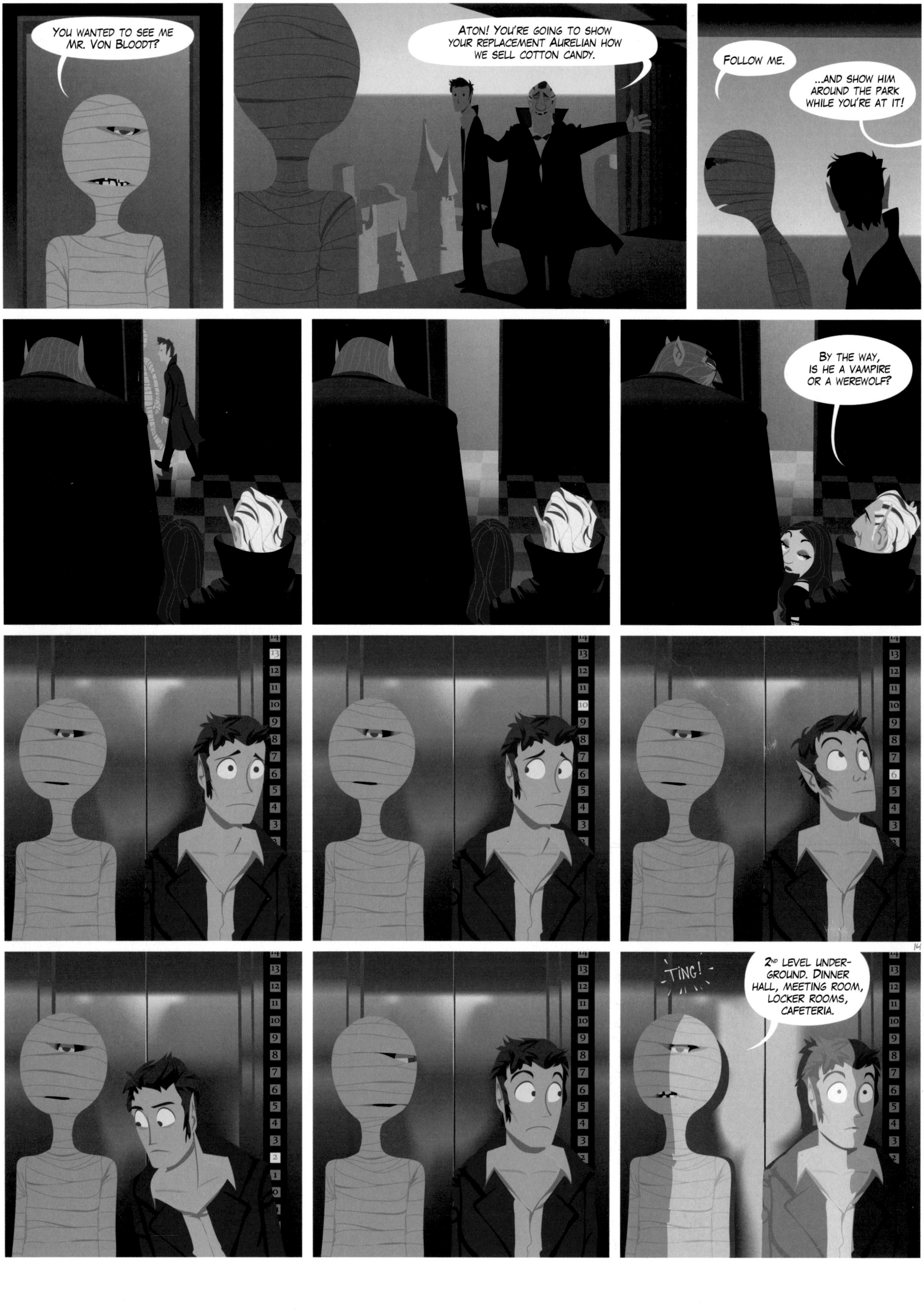
You wanted to see me Mr. Von Bloodt?
Aton! You're going to show your replacement Aurelian how we sell cotton candy.
Follow me.
...and show him around the park while you're at it!
By the way, is he a vampire or a werewolf?
TING!
2nd level underground. Dinner hall, meeting room, locker rooms, cafeteria.

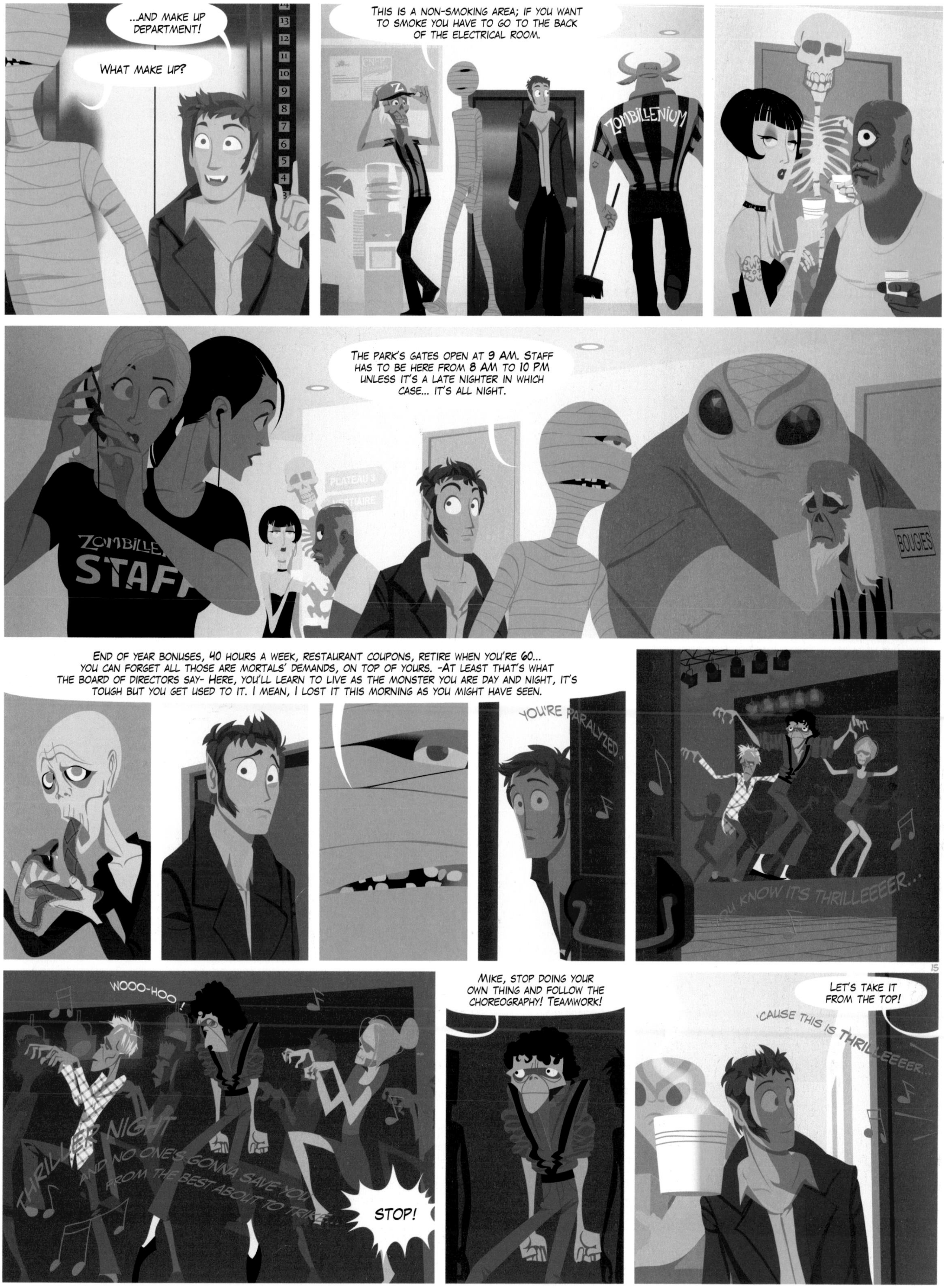

...AND MAKE UP DEPARTMENT!
WHAT MAKE UP?
THIS IS A NON-SMOKING AREA; IF YOU WANT TO SMOKE YOU HAVE TO GO TO THE BACK OF THE ELECTRICAL ROOM.
ZOMBILLENIUM
THE PARK'S GATES OPEN AT 9 AM. STAFF HAS TO BE HERE FROM 8 AM TO 10 PM UNLESS IT'S A LATE NIGHTER IN WHICH CASE... IT'S ALL NIGHT.
ZOMBILLEN
STAFF
PLATEAU 3
VESTIAIRE
BOUGIES
END OF YEAR BONUSES, 40 HOURS A WEEK, RESTAURANT COUPONS, RETIRE WHEN YOU'RE 60... YOU CAN FORGET ALL THOSE ARE MORTALS' DEMANDS, ON TOP OF YOURS. -AT LEAST THAT'S WHAT THE BOARD OF DIRECTORS SAY- HERE, YOU'LL LEARN TO LIVE AS THE MONSTER YOU ARE DAY AND NIGHT, IT'S TOUGH BUT YOU GET USED TO IT. I MEAN, I LOST IT THIS MORNING AS YOU MIGHT HAVE SEEN.
YOU'RE PARALYZED...
YOU KNOW IT'S THRILLEEEER...
WOOO-HOO!
THRILLER NIGHT
AND NO ONE'S GONNA SAVE YOU FROM THE BEST ABOUT TO TRIKE...
STOP!
MIKE, STOP DOING YOUR OWN THING AND FOLLOW THE CHOREOGRAPHY! TEAMWORK!
LET'S TAKE IT FROM THE TOP!
'CAUSE THIS IS THRILLEEEER...

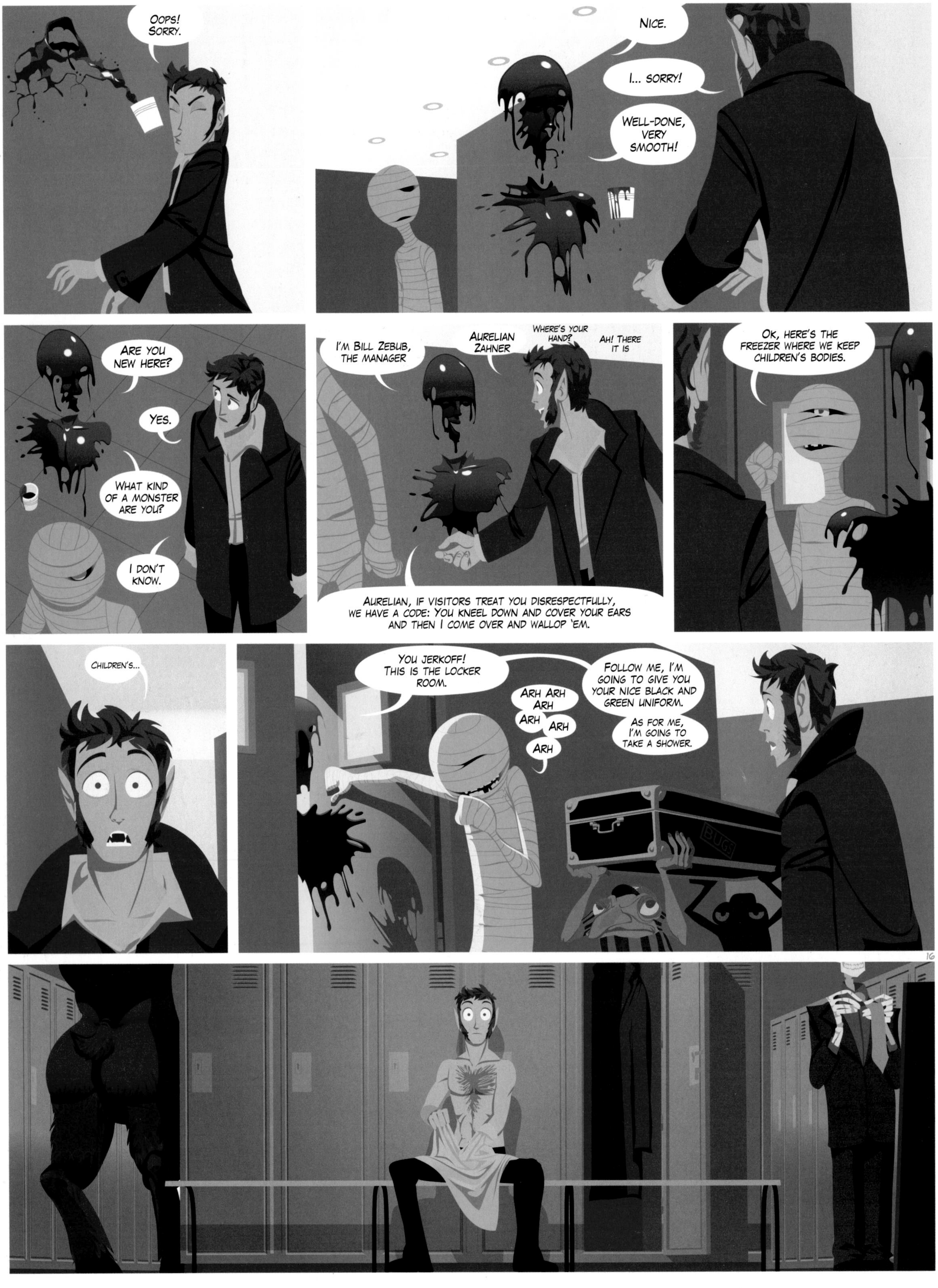

Oops! Sorry.
Nice.
I... sorry!
Well-done, very smooth!
Are you new here?
Yes.
What kind of a monster are you?
I don't know.
I'm Bill Zebub, the manager
Aurelian Zahner
Where's your hand?
Ah! There it is
Aurelian, if visitors treat you disrespectfully, we have a code: You kneel down and cover your ears and then I come over and wallop 'em.
Ok, here's the freezer where we keep children's bodies.
Children's...
You jerkoff! This is the locker room.
Arh arh arh
Arh
Arh
Arh
Follow me, I'm going to give you your nice black and green uniform.
As for me, I'm going to take a shower.
BUGS

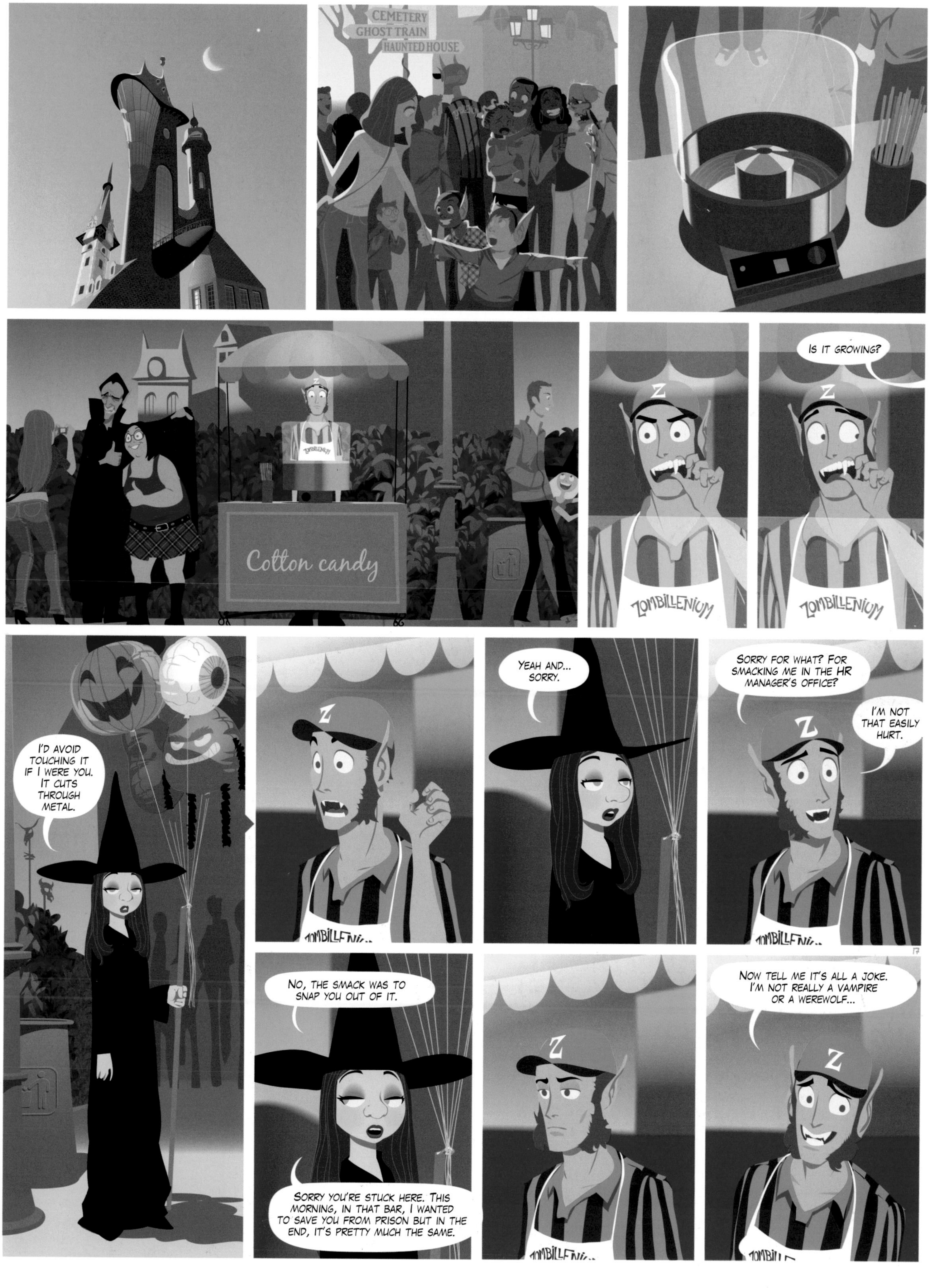
CEMETERY
GHOST TRAIN
HAUNTED HOUSE
ZOMBILLENIUM
Cotton candy
ZOMBILLENIUM
IS IT GROWING?
ZOMBILLENIUM
I'D AVOID TOUCHING IT IF I WERE YOU. IT CUTS THROUGH METAL.
YEAH AND... SORRY.
SORRY FOR WHAT? FOR SMACKING ME IN THE HR MANAGER'S OFFICE?
I'M NOT THAT EASILY HURT.
NO, THE SMACK WAS TO SNAP YOU OUT OF IT.
SORRY YOU'RE STUCK HERE. THIS MORNING, IN THAT BAR, I WANTED TO SAVE YOU FROM PRISON BUT IN THE END, IT'S PRETTY MUCH THE SAME.
NOW TELL ME IT'S ALL A JOKE. I'M NOT REALLY A VAMPIRE OR A WEREWOLF...

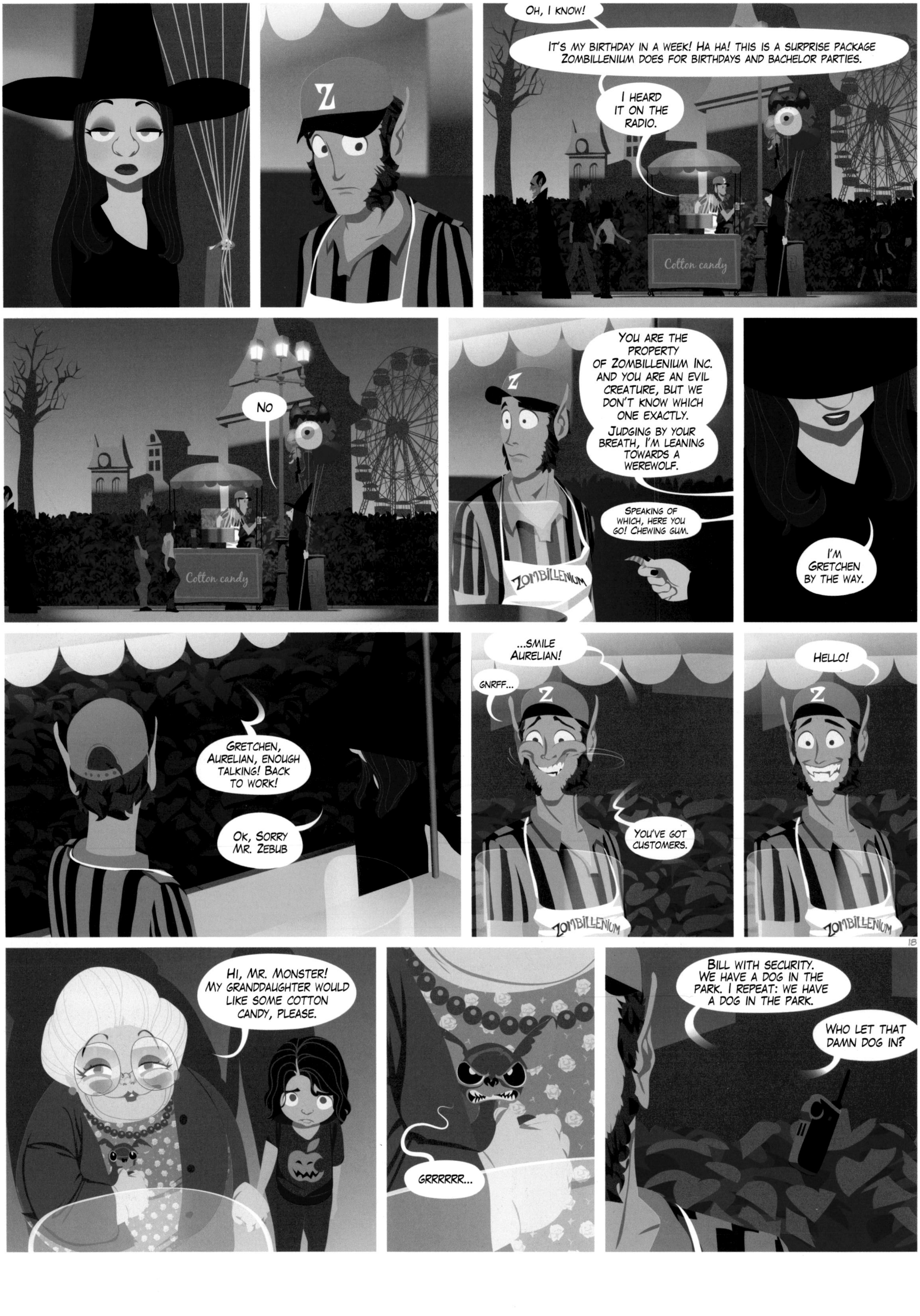

Oh, I know!
It's my birthday in a week! Ha ha! This is a surprise package Zombillenium does for birthdays and bachelor parties.
I heard it on the radio.
Cotton candy
No
Cotton candy
You are the property of Zombillenium Inc. and you are an evil creature, but we don't know which one exactly. Judging by your breath, I'm leaning towards a werewolf.
Speaking of which, here you go! Chewing gum.
Zombillenium
I'm Gretchen by the way.
Gretchen, Aurelian, enough talking! Back to work!
Ok, sorry Mr. Zebub
...smile Aurelian!
Gnrff...
You've got customers.
Zombillenium
Hello!
Zombillenium
Hi, Mr. Monster! My granddaughter would like some cotton candy, please.
Grrrrrr...
Bill with security. We have a dog in the park. I repeat: we have a dog in the park.
Who let that damn dog in?

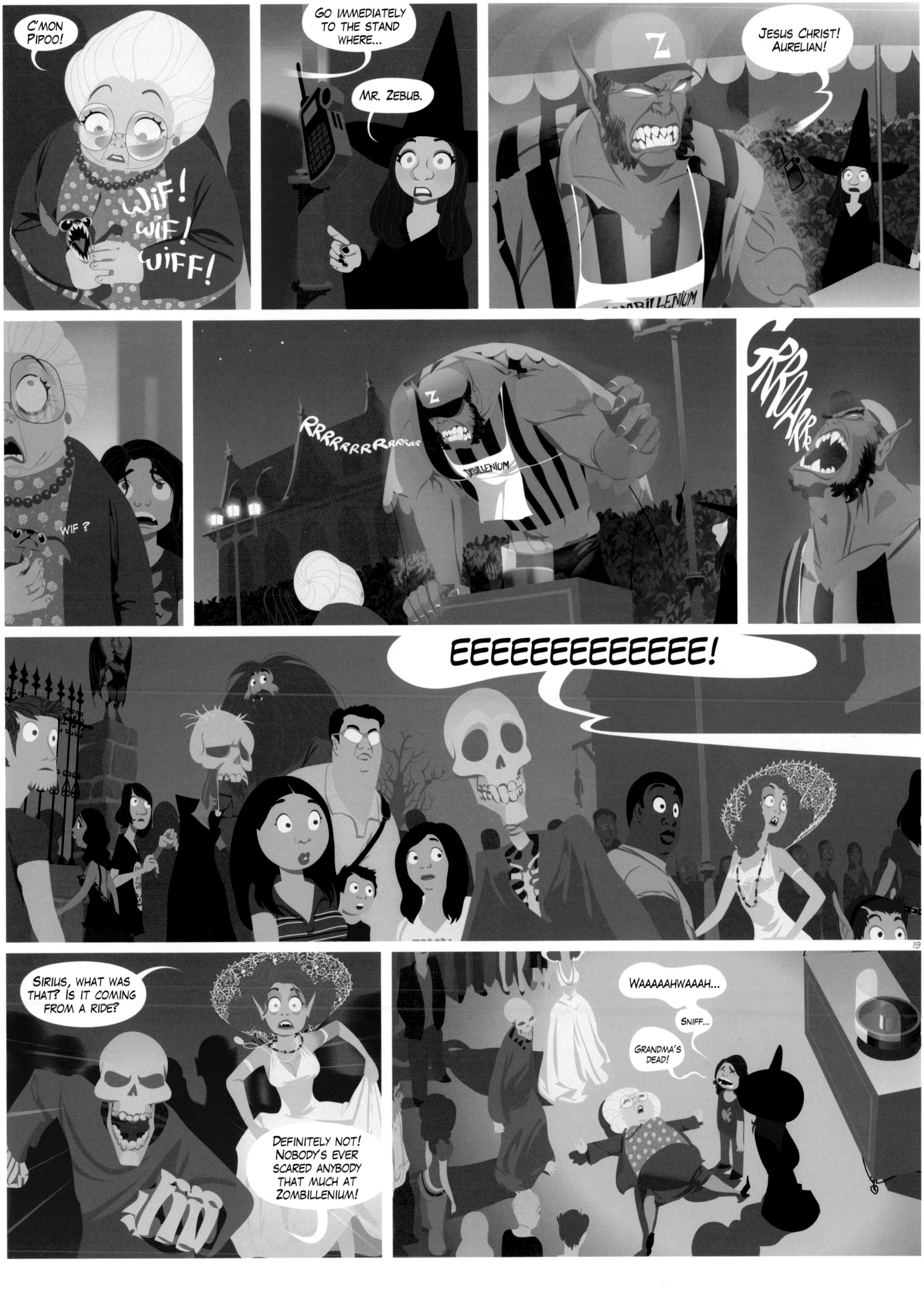
C'MON PIPOO!
WIF! WIF! WIFF!
GO IMMEDIATELY TO THE STAND WHERE...
MR. ZEBUB.
JESUS CHRIST! AURELIAN!
ZOMBILLENIUM
WIF ?
RRRRRRRRRRRRR
ZOMBILLENIUM
GRROARR
EEEEEEEEEEEEEE!
SIRIUS, WHAT WAS THAT? IS IT COMING FROM A RIDE?
DEFINITELY NOT! NOBODY'S EVER SCARED ANYBODY THAT MUCH AT ZOMBILLENIUM!
WAAAAAHWAAAH...
SNIFF...
GRANDMA'S DEAD!

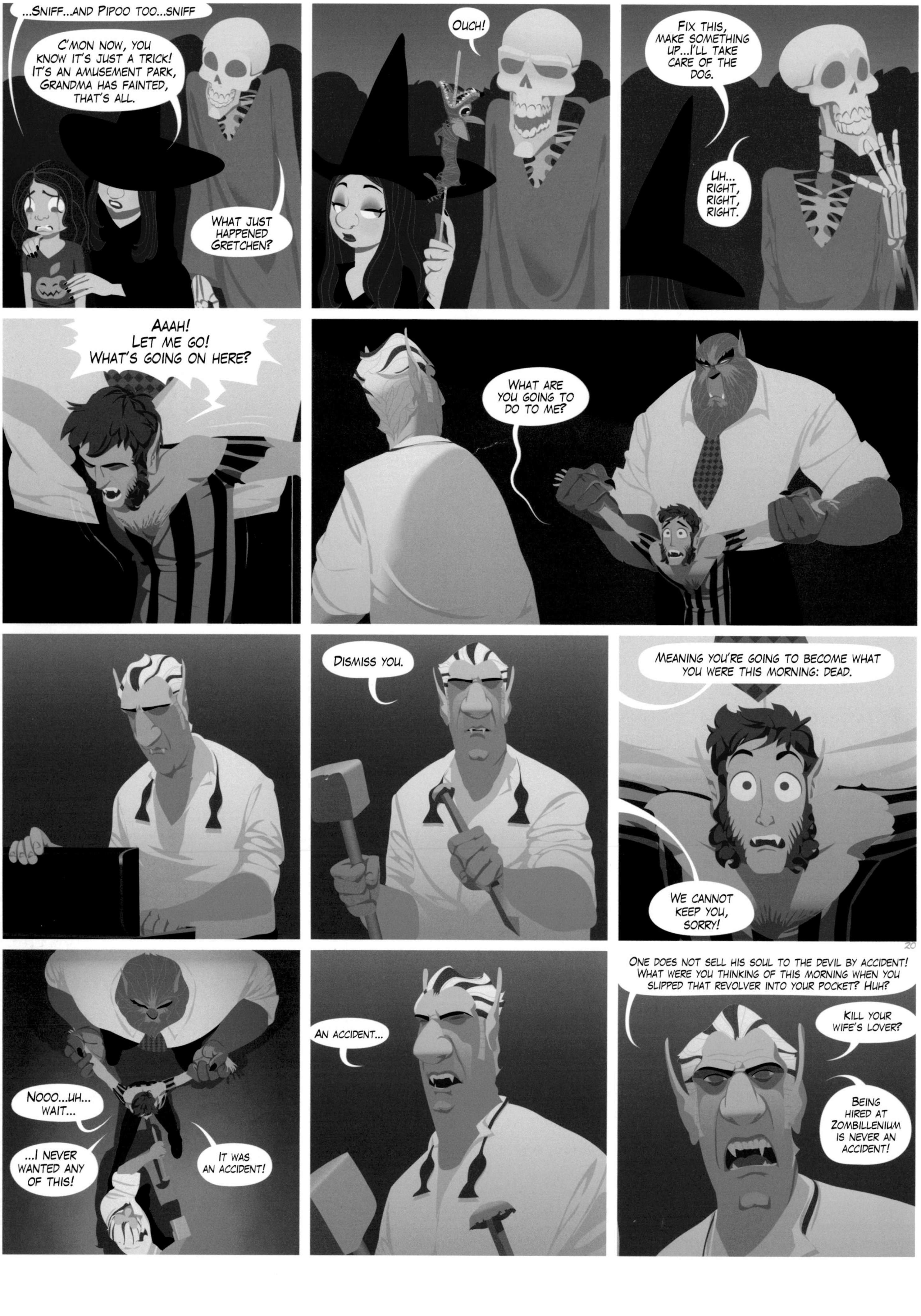
...Sniff...and Pipoo too...sniff
C'mon now, you know it's just a trick! It's an amusement park, Grandma has fainted, that's all.
What just happened Gretchen?
Ouch!
Fix this, make something up...I'll take care of the dog.
Uh... right, right, right.
Aaah! Let me go! What's going on here?
What are you going to do to me?
Dismiss you.
Meaning you're going to become what you were this morning: dead.
We cannot keep you, sorry!
Nooo...uh... wait...
...I never wanted any of this!
It was an accident!
An accident...
One does not sell his soul to the devil by accident! What were you thinking of this morning when you slipped that revolver into your pocket? Huh?
Kill your wife's lover?
Being hired at Zombillenium is never an accident!

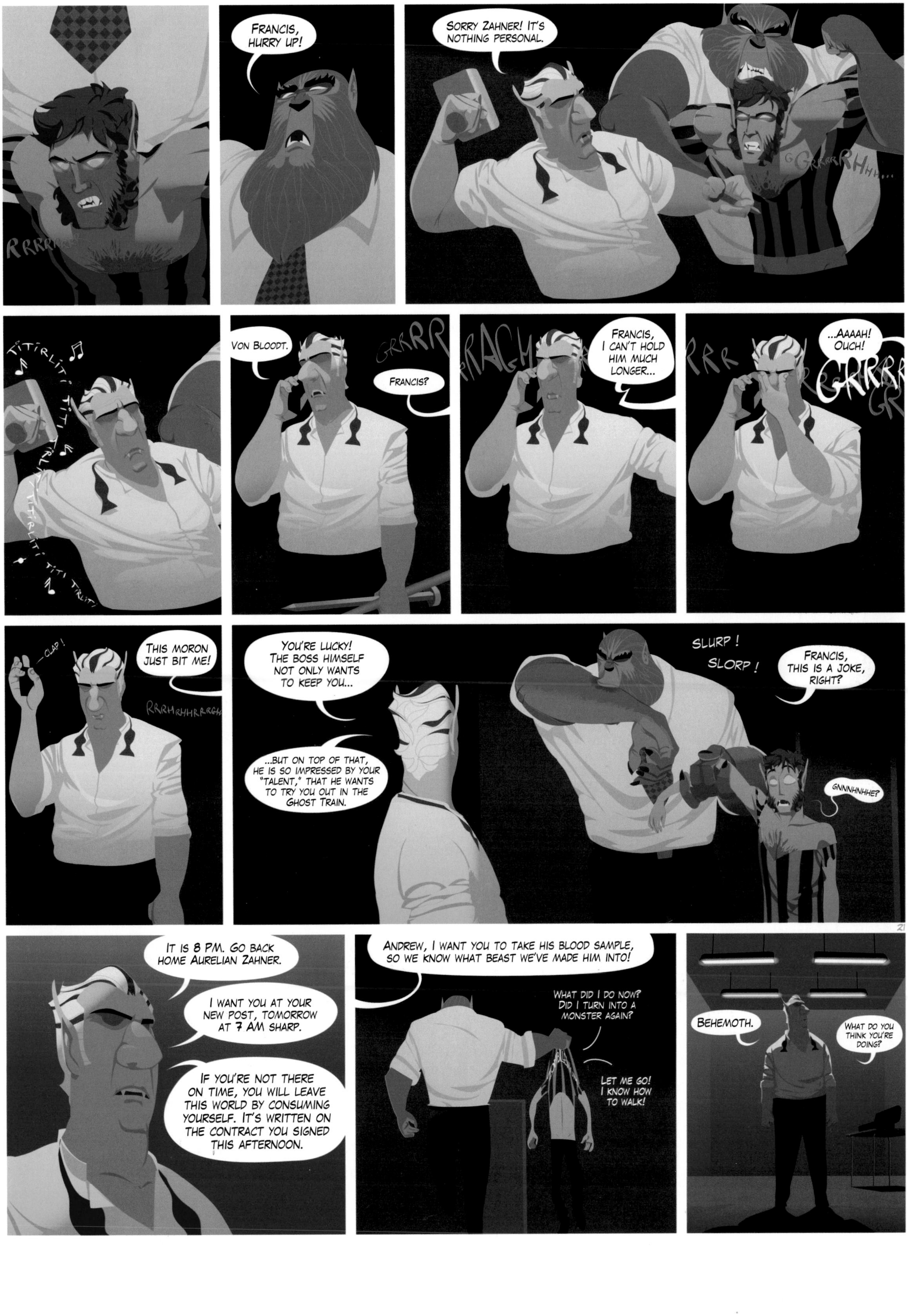

RRRRRRR
FRANCIS, HURRY UP!
SORRY ZAHNER! IT'S NOTHING PERSONAL.
GRRRRRHHH...
TITIRLITI TITI TIRLITI TITIRLITI TITI TIRLITI
VON BLOODT.
GRRRR
FRANCIS?
RRAGH
FRANCIS, I CAN'T HOLD HIM MUCH LONGER...
RRR
...AAAAH! OUCH!
GRRRR
CLAP!
THIS MORON JUST BIT ME!
RRRHRHHRRRGH
YOU'RE LUCKY! THE BOSS HIMSELF NOT ONLY WANTS TO KEEP YOU...
...BUT ON TOP OF THAT, HE IS SO IMPRESSED BY YOUR "TALENT," THAT HE WANTS TO TRY YOU OUT IN THE GHOST TRAIN.
SLURP!
SLORP!
FRANCIS, THIS IS A JOKE, RIGHT?
GNNNHNHHE?
IT IS 8 PM. GO BACK HOME AURELIAN ZAHNER.
I WANT YOU AT YOUR NEW POST, TOMORROW AT 7 AM SHARP.
IF YOU'RE NOT THERE ON TIME, YOU WILL LEAVE THIS WORLD BY CONSUMING YOURSELF. IT'S WRITTEN ON THE CONTRACT YOU SIGNED THIS AFTERNOON.
ANDREW, I WANT YOU TO TAKE HIS BLOOD SAMPLE, SO WE KNOW WHAT BEAST WE'VE MADE HIM INTO!
WHAT DID I DO NOW? DID I TURN INTO A MONSTER AGAIN?
LET ME GO! I KNOW HOW TO WALK!
BEHEMOTH.
WHAT DO YOU THINK YOU'RE DOING?

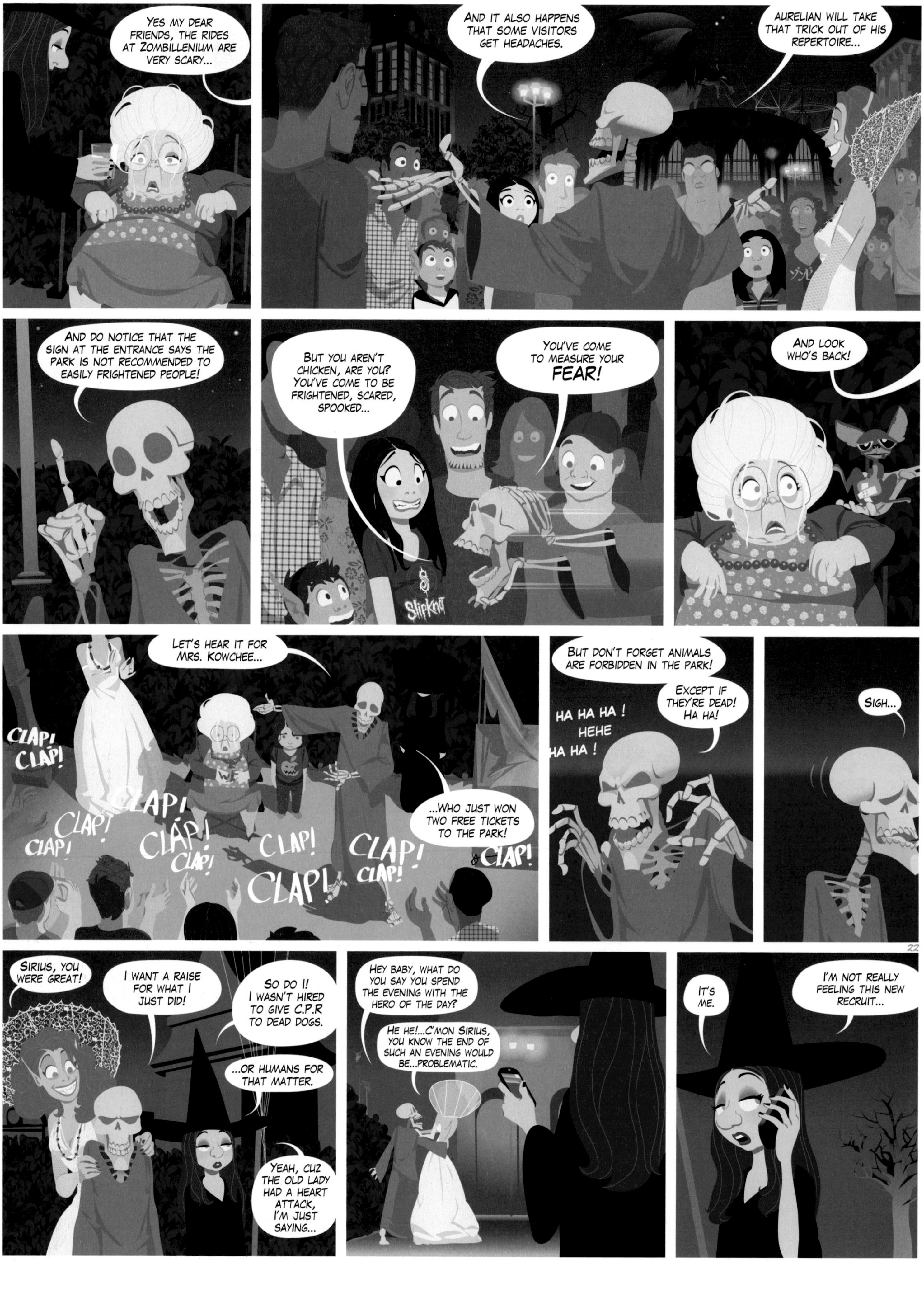
Yes my dear friends, the rides at Zombillenium are very scary...
And it also happens that some visitors get headaches.
Aurelian will take that trick out of his repertoire...
And do notice that the sign at the entrance says the park is not recommended to easily frightened people!
But you aren't chicken, are you? You've come to be frightened, scared, spooked...
You've come to measure your FEAR!
Slipknot
And look who's back!
Let's hear it for Mrs. Kowchee...
CLAP! CLAP!
CLAP! CLAP! CLAP! CLAP! CLAP! CLAP! CLAP! CLAP! CLAP! CLAP! CLAP!
...who just won two free tickets to the park!
But don't forget animals are forbidden in the park!
Except if they're dead! Ha ha!
HA HA HA ! HEHE HA HA !
Sigh...
Sirius, you were great!
I want a raise for what I just did!
So do I! I wasn't hired to give C.P.R to dead dogs.
...or humans for that matter.
Yeah, cuz the old lady had a heart attack, I'm just saying...
Hey baby, what do you say you spend the evening with the hero of the day?
He he!...C'mon Sirius, you know the end of such an evening would be...problematic.
It's me.
I'm not really feeling this new recruit...

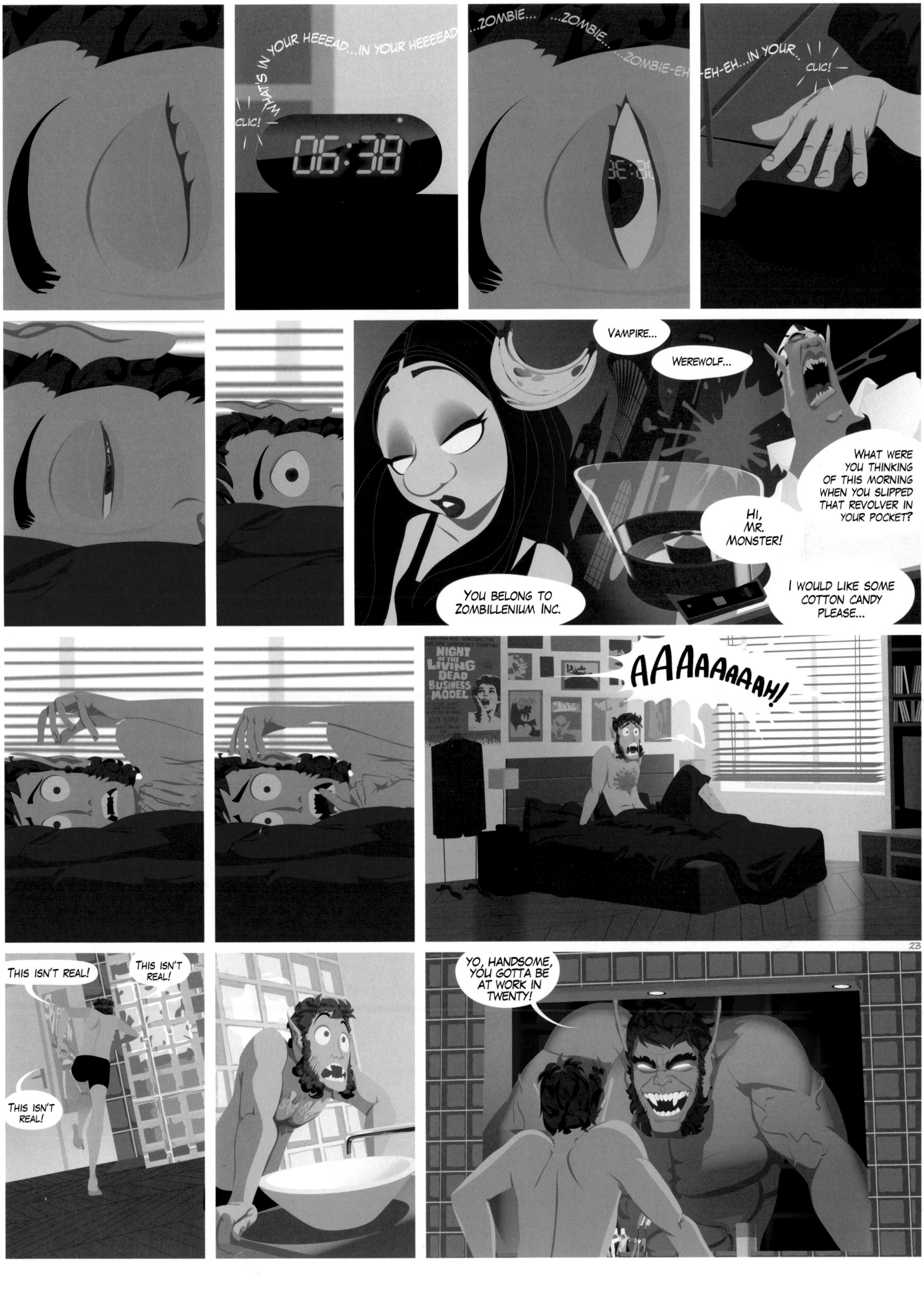
CLIC!
WHAT'S IN YOUR HEEEAD...IN YOUR HEEEEAD...
06:38
...ZOMBIE... ...ZOMBIE...
...ZOMBIE-EH-EH-EH...IN YOUR...
CLIC!
VAMPIRE...
WEREWOLF...
WHAT WERE YOU THINKING OF THIS MORNING WHEN YOU SLIPPED THAT REVOLVER IN YOUR POCKET?
HI, MR. MONSTER!
YOU BELONG TO ZOMBILLENIUM INC.
I WOULD LIKE SOME COTTON CANDY PLEASE...
NIGHT OF THE LIVING DEAD BUSINESS MODEL
AAAAAAAAH!
THIS ISN'T REAL!
THIS ISN'T REAL!
THIS ISN'T REAL!
YO, HANDSOME, YOU GOTTA BE AT WORK IN TWENTY!

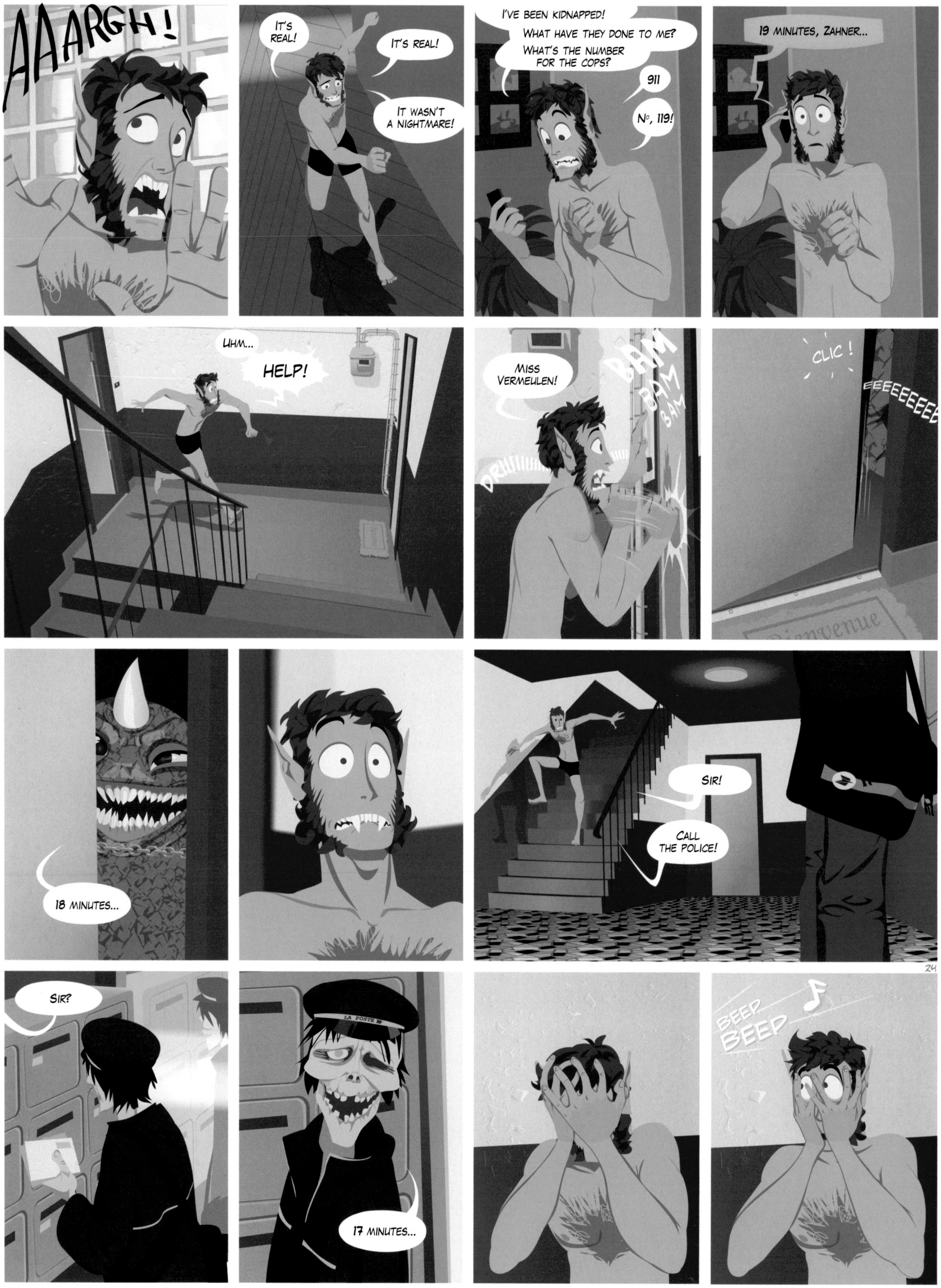
AAARGH!
It's real!
It's real!
It wasn't a nightmare!
I've been kidnapped!
What have they done to me?
What's the number for the cops?
911
No, 119!
19 minutes, Zahner...
Uhm...
HELP!
Miss Vermeulen!
BAM
BAM
BAM
CLIC!
EEEEEEEEB
Bienvenue
18 minutes...
Sir!
Call the police!
Sir?
LA POSTE
17 minutes...
BEEP
BEEP

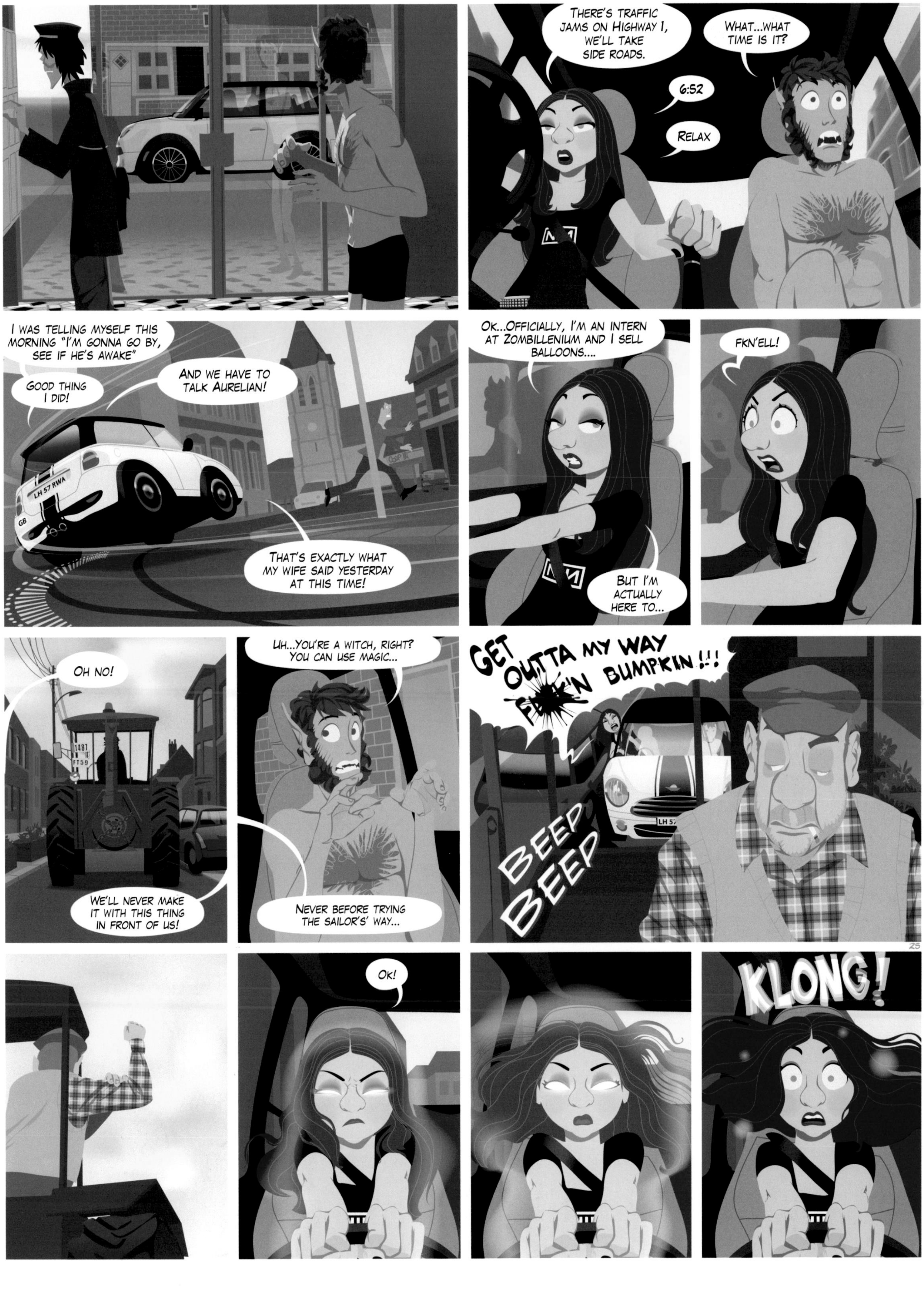
There's traffic jams on Highway 1, we'll take side roads.
What...what time is it?
6:52
Relax
I was telling myself this morning "I'm gonna go by, see if he's awake"
Good thing I did!
And we have to talk Aurelian!
That's exactly what my wife said yesterday at this time!
Ok...Officially, I'm an intern at Zombillenium and I sell balloons....
But I'm actually here to...
Fkn'ell!
Oh no!
We'll never make it with this thing in front of us!
Uh...you're a witch, right? You can use magic...
Never before trying the sailor's' way...
Get outta my way F**'n bumpkin!!!
Beep Beep
Ok!
Klong!

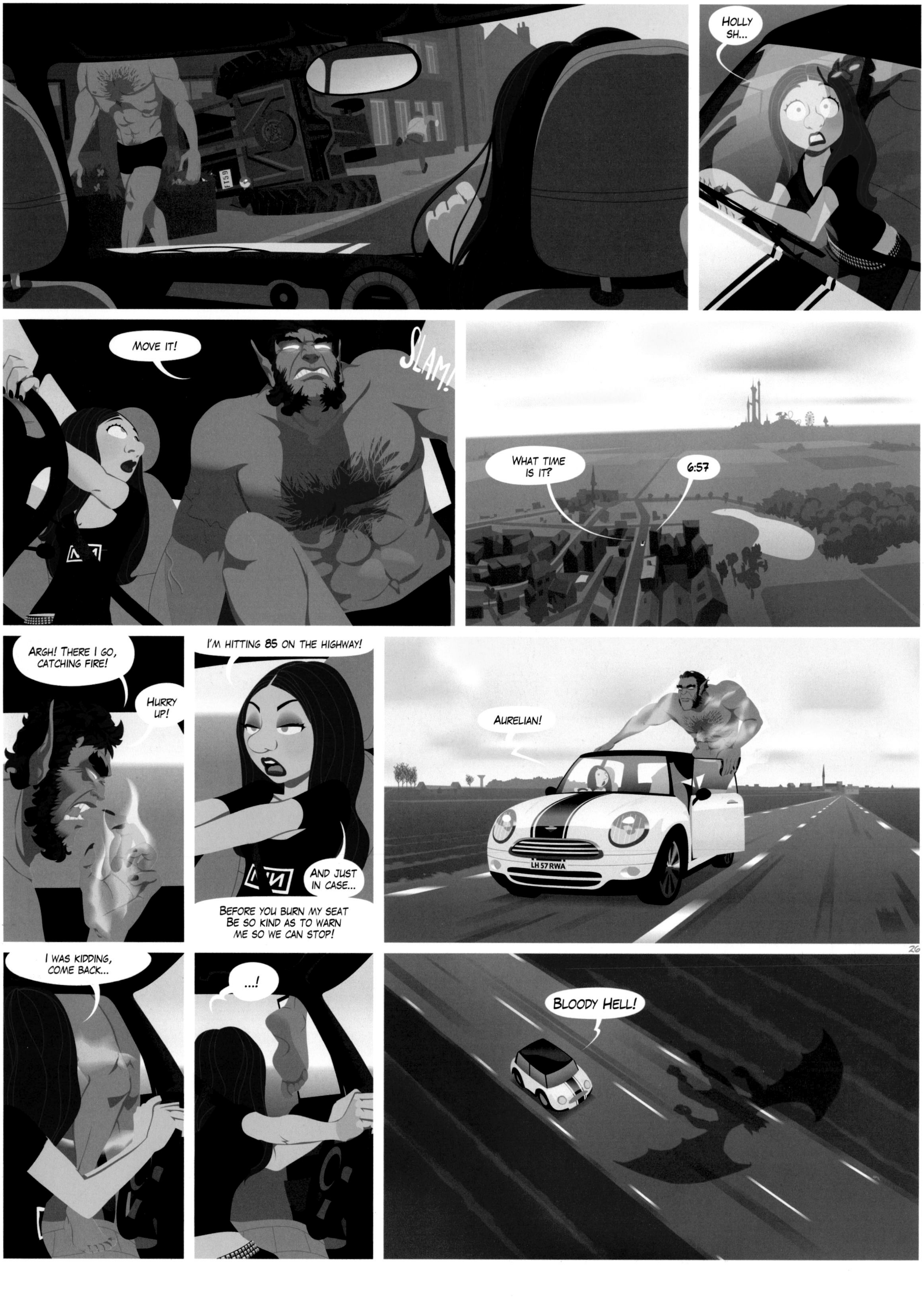

Holly sh...
Move it!
Slam!
What time is it?
6:57
Argh! There I go, catching fire!
Hurry up!
I'm hitting 85 on the highway!
And just in case...
Before you burn my seat Be so kind as to warn me so we can stop!
Aurelian!
LH 57 RWA
I was kidding, come back...
...!
Bloody Hell!

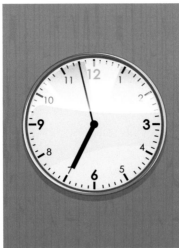

HEY! ATON! NO BLOOD, THERE ARE HUMANS AT THE TABLE.

ATON! IS ZAHNER HERE?

NOT THAT I KNOW OF.

AHEM! LADIES, GENTLEMEN. SHALL WE BEGIN?

OK.

AS A LEGAL REPRESENTATIVE OF MR. BEHEMOTH'S INTERESTS THROUGH HIS EN-HELL-TAINMENT COMPANY COMPRISED OF 9 THEME PARKS, 32 CASINOS AND 54 CLUBS AROUND THE WORLD, AS WELL AS 51 OF THE SHARES OF THIS AMUSEMENT PARK...

...I HAVE THE HONOR OF OPENING THIS GENERAL MEETING WITH THE SHAREHOLDERS OF ZOMBILLENIUM INC. TO QUOTE MR. BEHEMOTH'S FAVORITE EXPRESSION: THERE WILL BE BLOOD.

OUR PARK IS BANKRUPT WITH A HUGE BUDGET DEFICIT AND WE ARE NUMBER EIGHTEEN IN THE TOP TWENTY LARGEST AMUSEMENT PARKS IN THE COUNTRY...FAR BEHIND DISNEYLAND, SEAWORLD AND KNOTS BERRY FARM, OBVIOUSLY; BUT I MUST TELL YOU WE HAVE THE SAD PRIVILEGE OF BEING BEHIND VULCANA.

WE'RE IN A RECESSION... WHY WOULD PEOPLE GO SEE ZOMBIES ON A WEEKEND WHEN THEY HAVE TO SEE THEIR BOSS ALL WEEK?

WELL! YOU WOULDN'T COME TO MIND!

FRANCIS!

WHY DON'T YOU JUST SAY IT? UNIONS! DO YOU KNOW WHAT IT WOULD MEAN TO DISMISS AN EMPLOYEE AT ZOMBILLENIUM?

FRANCIS, WE'RE NOT THERE YET!

I'M SURE OUR SHAREHOLDER FRIENDS HAVE PLENTY OF IDEAS, DON'T THEY?

YES! WE MUST SCARE THEM!

YOUNG KIDS LOVE GORE, CRUELTY, BRUTALITY,... ZOMBIES ARE OLD NEWS!

YES, SOME RIDES ARE TOTALLY BORING!

MOST OF THE VISITORS ARE GOTHS. DO YOU KNOW THE PURCHASING POWER OF A GOTH?...EL ZILCHO!

PEOPLE ARE FALLING ASLEEP IN THE GHOST TRAIN!

WHAT ABOUT A PARK WHERE THEY ARE TRAPPED AND THEY HAVE TO FIGHT EACH OTHER TO GET OUT?

BUT ABOVE ALL, WE MUST CUT BACK!

CUSTOMERS AREN'T COMING TO BE SCARED ANYMORE BUT TO GET A LAUGH OUT OF IT!

WE NO LONGER HAVE A CHOICE.

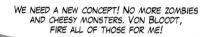

WE NEED A NEW CONCEPT! NO MORE ZOMBIES AND CHEESY MONSTERS. VON BLOODT, FIRE ALL OF THOSE FOR ME!

WE ARE GOING TO BE THE ONLY THEME PARK THAT'S ACTUALLY SCARY! AND TO LAUNCH THIS, WE NEED A MASCOT!

THE PRINCE OF DARKN...

FLAP FLAP FLAP FLAP

BLAF!

VON BLOODT, WHAT THE HELL IS THAT?

AN ON TIME EMPLOYEE, AVOIDING TERMINATION.

AND WHO CAN'T MASTER FLIGHT YET

MARVELOUS!

HERE'S MR. BEHEMOTH'S ACE UP THE SLEEVE!

THE DEVIL HIMSELF!

HOW COULD WE HAVE MISSED IT?!

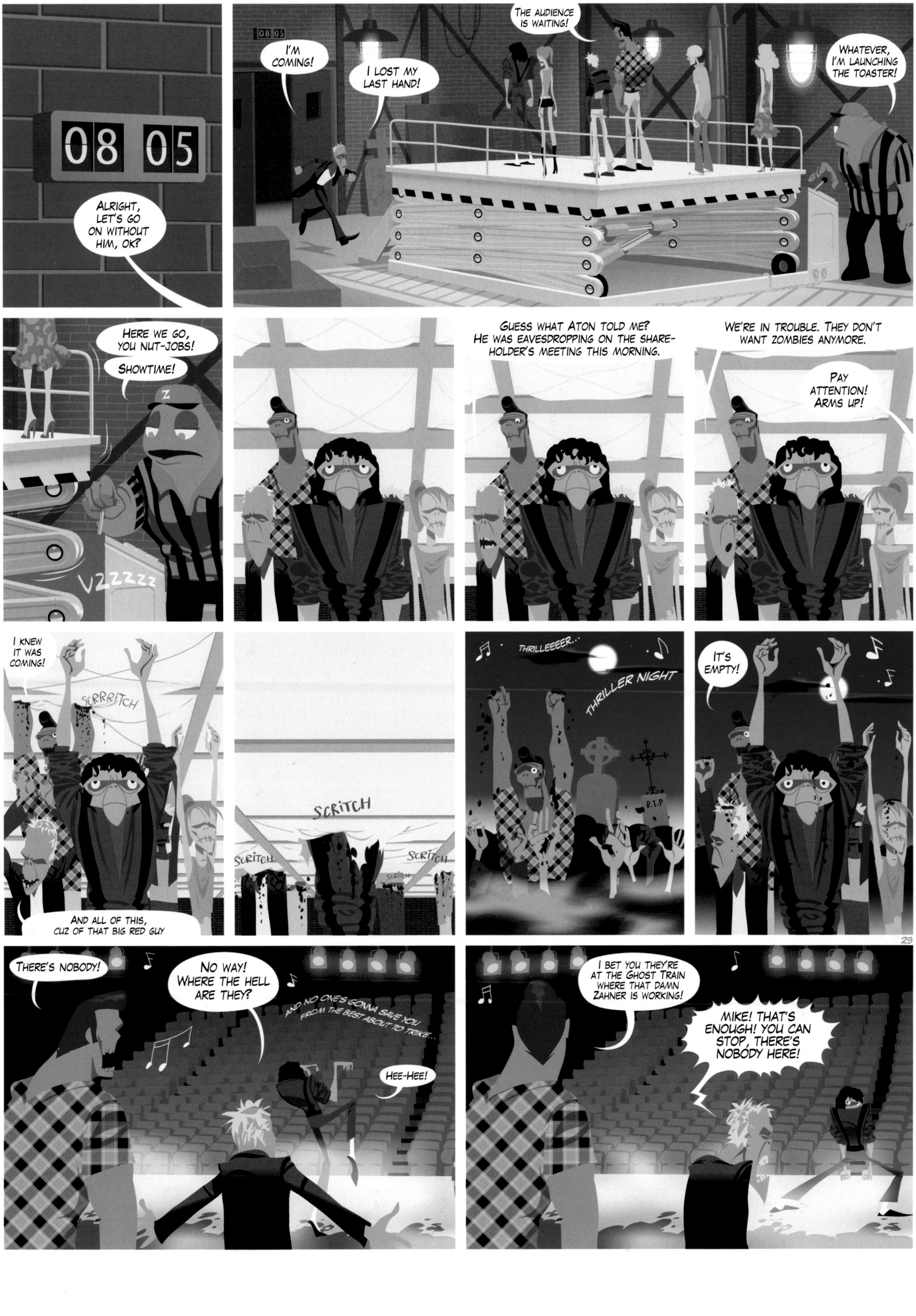
08 05
Alright, let's go on without him, ok?
08 05
I'm coming!
I lost my last hand!
The audience is waiting!
Whatever, I'm launching the toaster!
Here we go, you nut-jobs!
Showtime!
Vzzzzz
Guess what Aton told me? He was eavesdropping on the share-holder's meeting this morning.
We're in trouble. They don't want zombies anymore.
Pay attention! Arms up!
I knew it was coming!
Scrrritch
And all of this, cuz of that big red guy
Scritch
Scritch
Scritch
Scritch
Thrilleeeer...
Thriller night
R.I.P
It's empty!
There's nobody!
No way! Where the hell are they?
And no one's gonna save you from the best about to trike...
Hee-Hee!
I bet you they're at the Ghost Train where that damn Zahner is working!
Mike! That's enough! You can stop, there's nobody here!

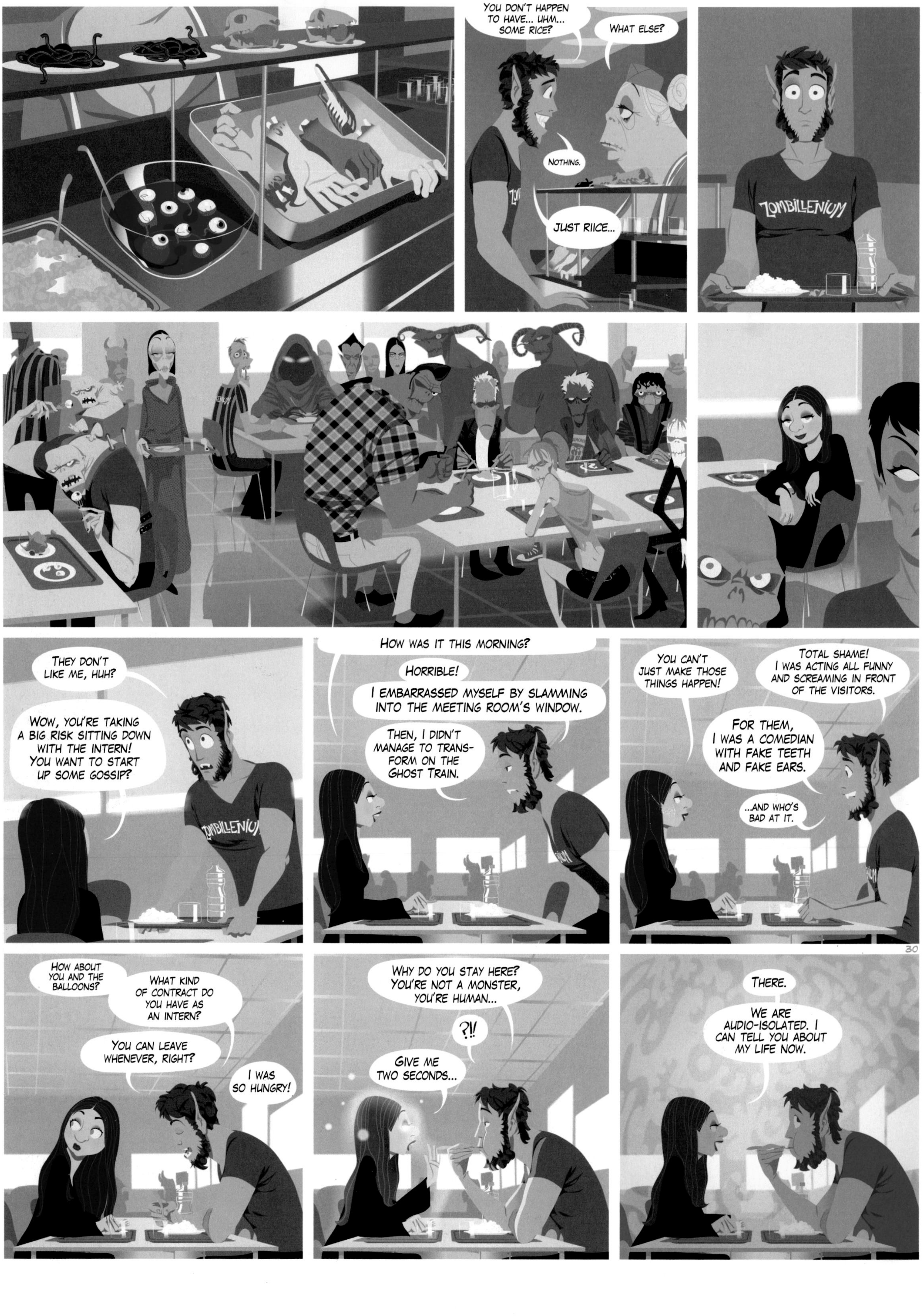

YOU DON'T HAPPEN TO HAVE... UHM... SOME RICE?
WHAT ELSE?
NOTHING.
JUST RIICE...
THEY DON'T LIKE ME, HUH?
WOW, YOU'RE TAKING A BIG RISK SITTING DOWN WITH THE INTERN! YOU WANT TO START UP SOME GOSSIP?
HOW WAS IT THIS MORNING?
HORRIBLE!
I EMBARRASSED MYSELF BY SLAMMING INTO THE MEETING ROOM'S WINDOW.
THEN, I DIDN'T MANAGE TO TRANS-FORM ON THE GHOST TRAIN.
YOU CAN'T JUST MAKE THOSE THINGS HAPPEN!
TOTAL SHAME! I WAS ACTING ALL FUNNY AND SCREAMING IN FRONT OF THE VISITORS.
FOR THEM, I WAS A COMEDIAN WITH FAKE TEETH AND FAKE EARS.
...AND WHO'S BAD AT IT.
HOW ABOUT YOU AND THE BALLOONS?
WHAT KIND OF CONTRACT DO YOU HAVE AS AN INTERN?
YOU CAN LEAVE WHENEVER, RIGHT?
I WAS SO HUNGRY!
WHY DO YOU STAY HERE? YOU'RE NOT A MONSTER, YOU'RE HUMAN...
?!
GIVE ME TWO SECONDS...
THERE.
WE ARE AUDIO-ISOLATED. I CAN TELL YOU ABOUT MY LIFE NOW.

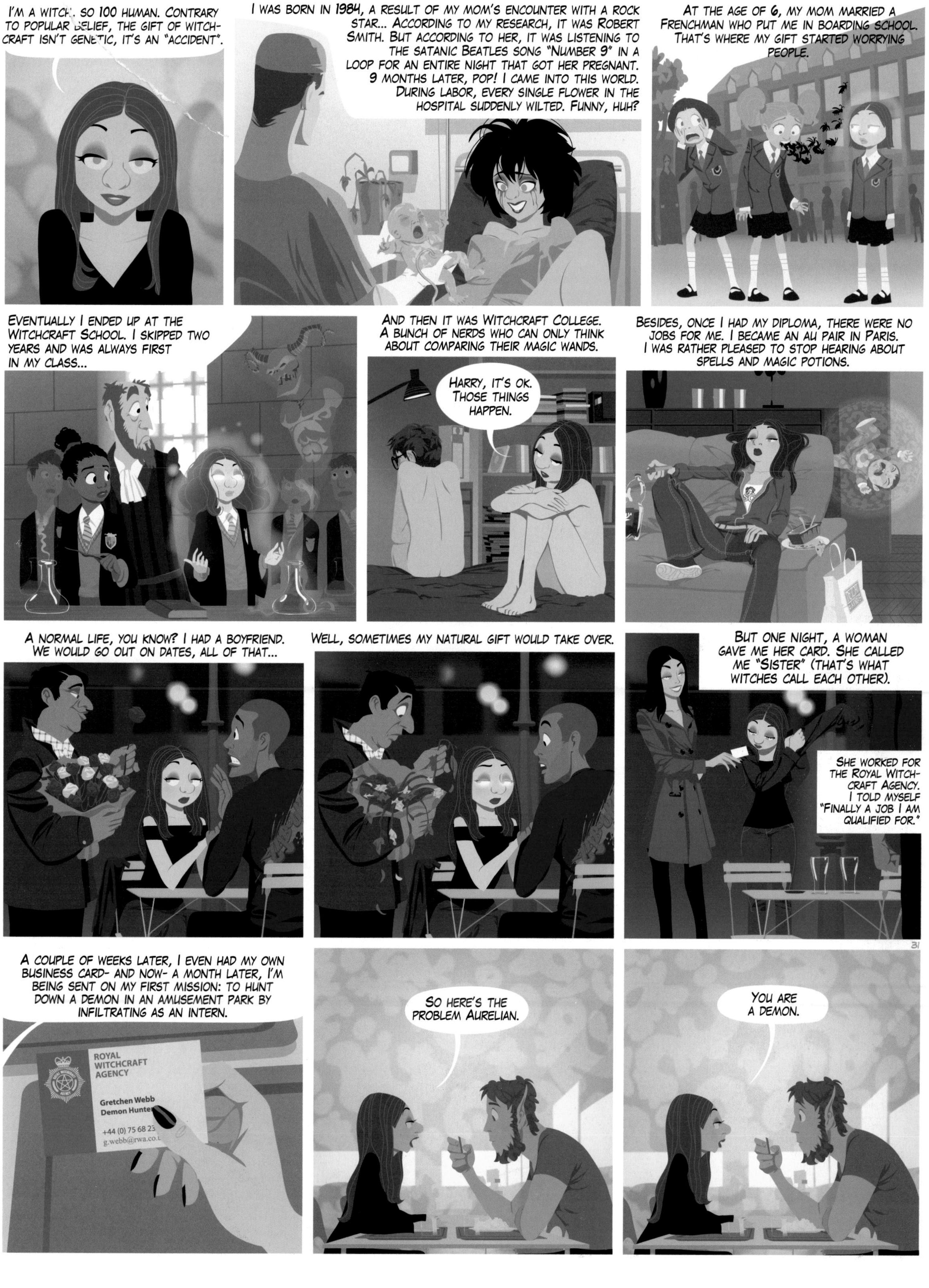
I'M A WITCH. SO 100 HUMAN. CONTRARY TO POPULAR BELIEF, THE GIFT OF WITCH-CRAFT ISN'T GENETIC, IT'S AN "ACCIDENT".
I WAS BORN IN 1984, A RESULT OF MY MOM'S ENCOUNTER WITH A ROCK STAR... ACCORDING TO MY RESEARCH, IT WAS ROBERT SMITH. BUT ACCORDING TO HER, IT WAS LISTENING TO THE SATANIC BEATLES SONG "NUMBER 9" IN A LOOP FOR AN ENTIRE NIGHT THAT GOT HER PREGNANT. 9 MONTHS LATER, POP! I CAME INTO THIS WORLD. DURING LABOR, EVERY SINGLE FLOWER IN THE HOSPITAL SUDDENLY WILTED. FUNNY, HUH?
AT THE AGE OF 6, MY MOM MARRIED A FRENCHMAN WHO PUT ME IN BOARDING SCHOOL. THAT'S WHERE MY GIFT STARTED WORRYING PEOPLE.
EVENTUALLY I ENDED UP AT THE WITCHCRAFT SCHOOL. I SKIPPED TWO YEARS AND WAS ALWAYS FIRST IN MY CLASS...
AND THEN IT WAS WITCHCRAFT COLLEGE. A BUNCH OF NERDS WHO CAN ONLY THINK ABOUT COMPARING THEIR MAGIC WANDS.
HARRY, IT'S OK. THOSE THINGS HAPPEN.
BESIDES, ONCE I HAD MY DIPLOMA, THERE WERE NO JOBS FOR ME. I BECAME AN AU PAIR IN PARIS. I WAS RATHER PLEASED TO STOP HEARING ABOUT SPELLS AND MAGIC POTIONS.
A NORMAL LIFE, YOU KNOW? I HAD A BOYFRIEND. WE WOULD GO OUT ON DATES, ALL OF THAT...
WELL, SOMETIMES MY NATURAL GIFT WOULD TAKE OVER.
BUT ONE NIGHT, A WOMAN GAVE ME HER CARD. SHE CALLED ME "SISTER" (THAT'S WHAT WITCHES CALL EACH OTHER).
SHE WORKED FOR THE ROYAL WITCH-CRAFT AGENCY. I TOLD MYSELF "FINALLY A JOB I AM QUALIFIED FOR."
A COUPLE OF WEEKS LATER, I EVEN HAD MY OWN BUSINESS CARD- AND NOW- A MONTH LATER, I'M BEING SENT ON MY FIRST MISSION: TO HUNT DOWN A DEMON IN AN AMUSEMENT PARK BY INFILTRATING AS AN INTERN.
ROYAL WITCHCRAFT AGENCY
Gretchen Webb
Demon Hunter
+44 (0) 75 68 23
g.webb@rwa.co.
SO HERE'S THE PROBLEM AURELIAN.
YOU ARE A DEMON.

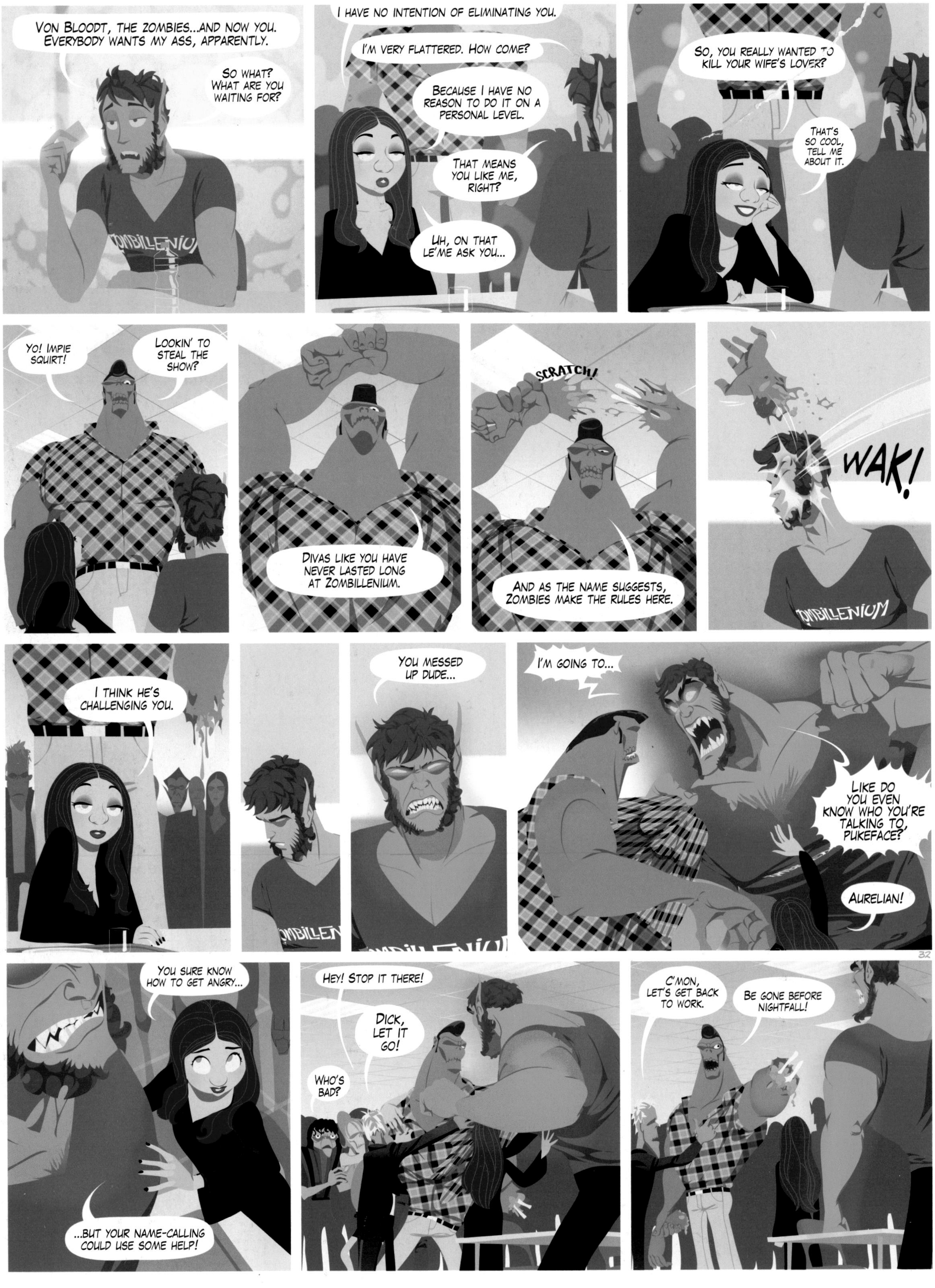
Von Bloodt, the zombies...and now you. Everybody wants my ass, apparently.
So what? What are you waiting for?
I have no intention of eliminating you.
I'm very flattered. How come?
Because I have no reason to do it on a personal level.
That means you like me, right?
Uh, on that le'me ask you...
So, you really wanted to kill your wife's lover?
That's so cool, tell me about it.
Yo! Impie squirt!
Lookin' to steal the show?
Divas like you have never lasted long at Zombillenium.
SCRATCH!
And as the name suggests, Zombies make the rules here.
WAK!
Zombillenium
I think he's challenging you.
You messed up dude...
I'm going to...
Like do you even know who you're talking to, pukeface?
Aurelian!
You sure know how to get angry...
...but your name-calling could use some help!
Hey! Stop it there!
Dick, let it go!
Who's bad?
C'mon, let's get back to work.
Be gone before nightfall!

32

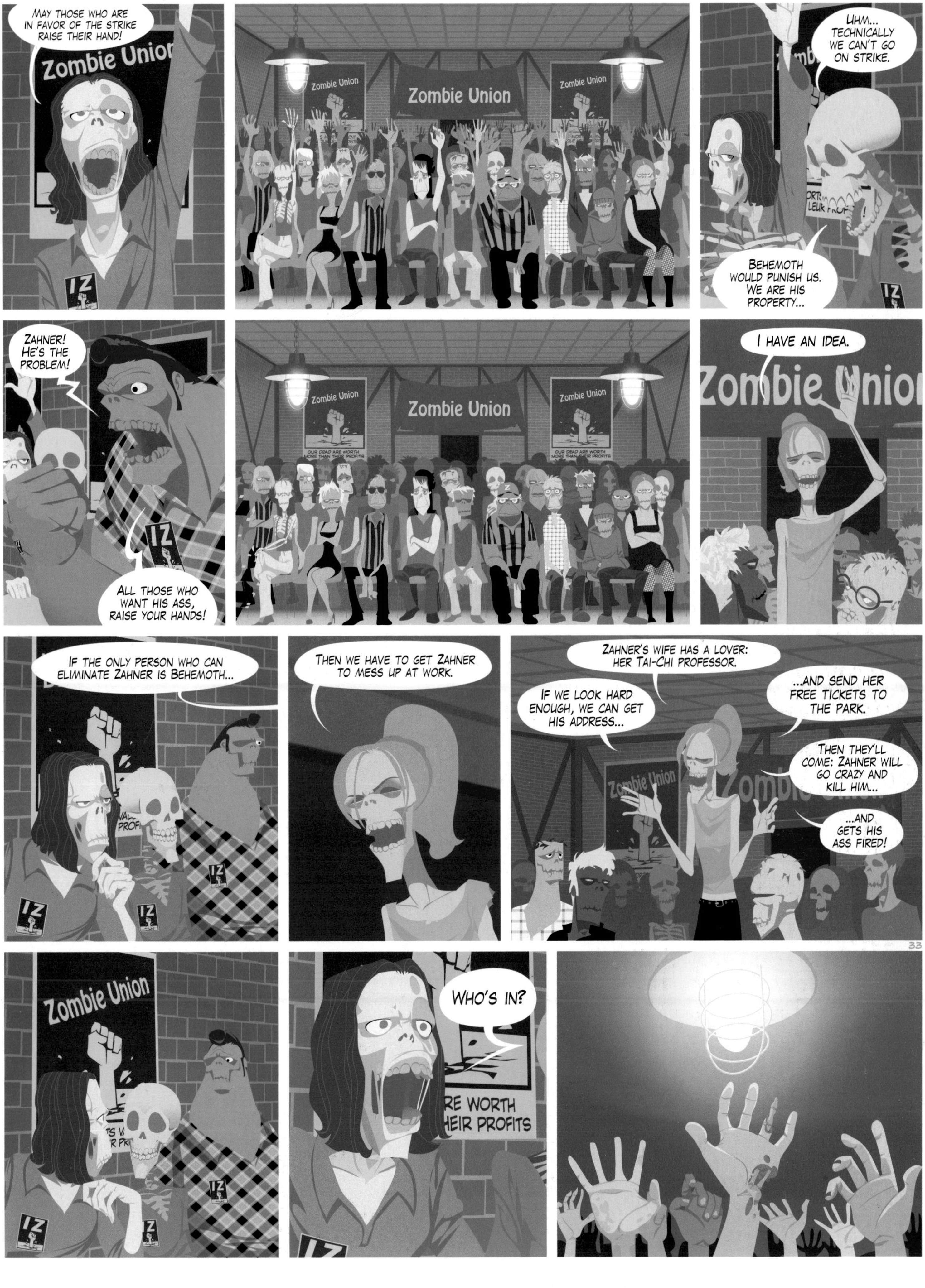

MAY THOSE WHO ARE IN FAVOR OF THE STRIKE RAISE THEIR HAND!
Zombie Union
Zombie Union
UHM... TECHNICALLY WE CAN'T GO ON STRIKE.
BEHEMOTH WOULD PUNISH US. WE ARE HIS PROPERTY...
ZAHNER! HE'S THE PROBLEM!
ALL THOSE WHO WANT HIS ASS, RAISE YOUR HANDS!
Zombie Union
I HAVE AN IDEA.
IF THE ONLY PERSON WHO CAN ELIMINATE ZAHNER IS BEHEMOTH...
THEN WE HAVE TO GET ZAHNER TO MESS UP AT WORK.
ZAHNER'S WIFE HAS A LOVER: HER TAI-CHI PROFESSOR.
IF WE LOOK HARD ENOUGH, WE CAN GET HIS ADDRESS...
...AND SEND HER FREE TICKETS TO THE PARK.
THEN THEY'LL COME: ZAHNER WILL GO CRAZY AND KILL HIM...
...AND GETS HIS ASS FIRED!
Zombie Union
WHO'S IN?
RE WORTH
HEIR PROFITS

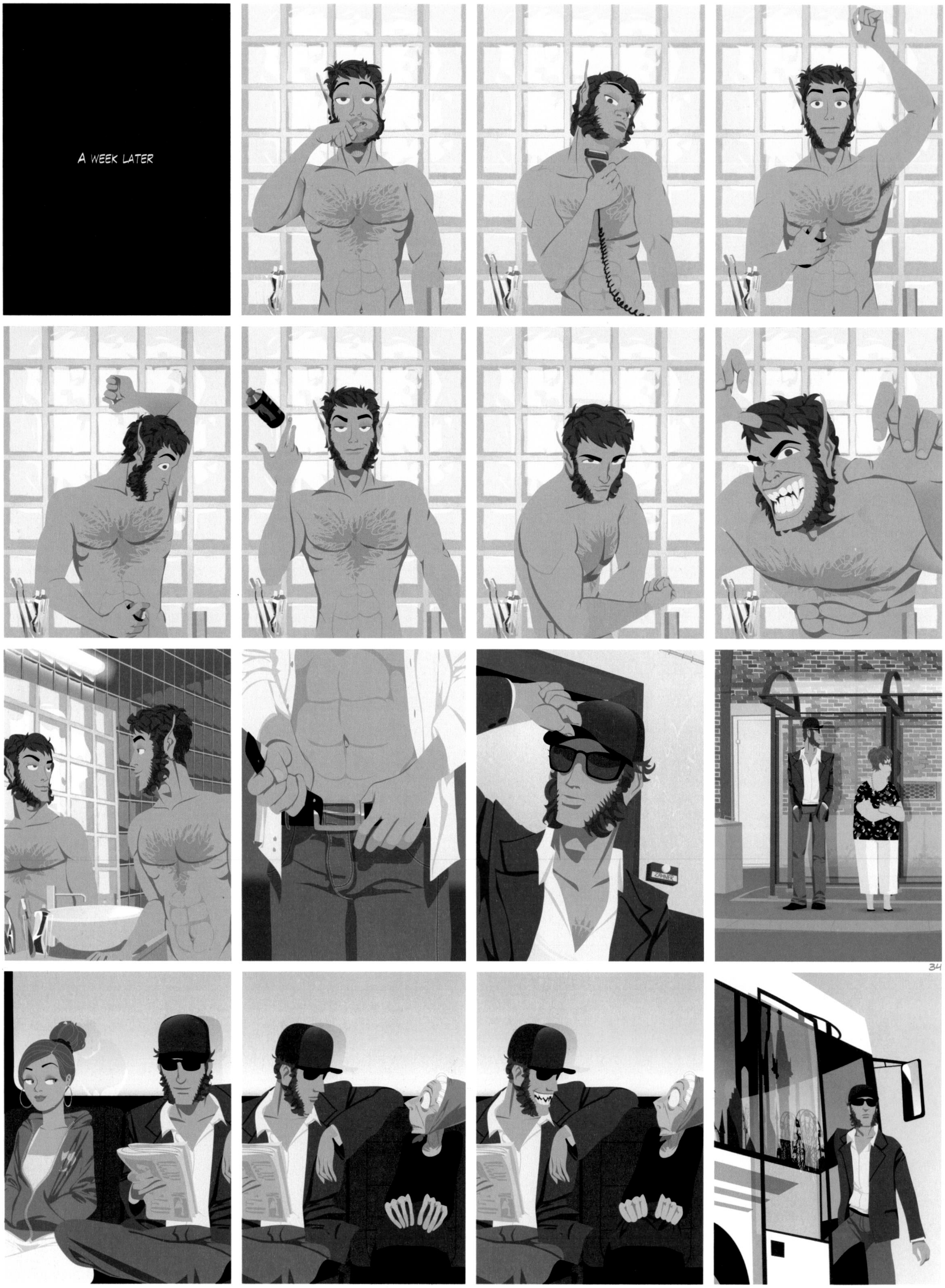
A WEEK LATER

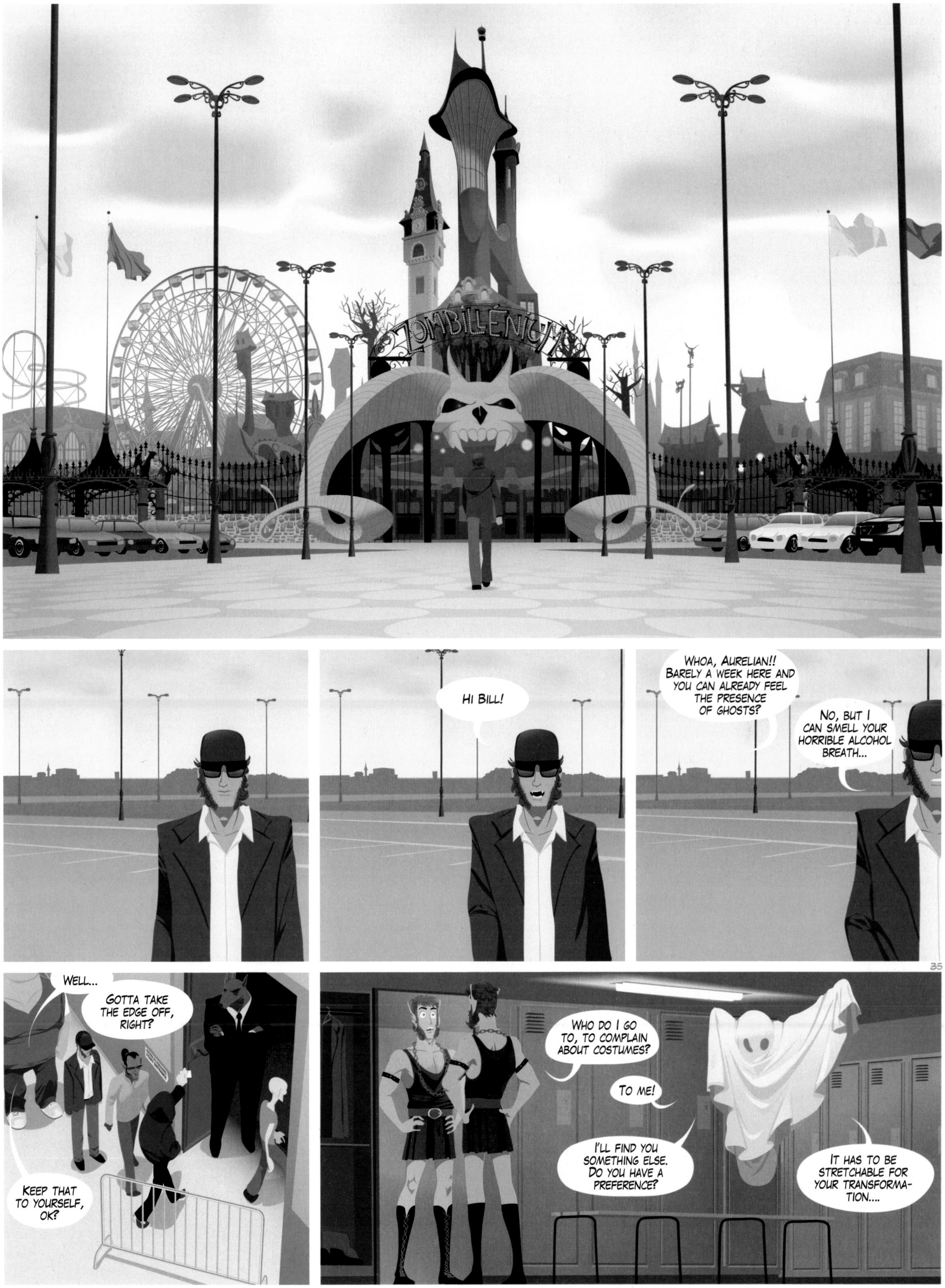
ZOMBILLÉNIUM
HI BILL!
WHOA, AURELIAN!! BARELY A WEEK HERE AND YOU CAN ALREADY FEEL THE PRESENCE OF GHOSTS?
NO, BUT I CAN SMELL YOUR HORRIBLE ALCOHOL BREATH...
WELL...
GOTTA TAKE THE EDGE OFF, RIGHT?
KEEP THAT TO YOURSELF, OK?
WHO DO I GO TO, TO COMPLAIN ABOUT COSTUMES?
TO ME!
I'LL FIND YOU SOMETHING ELSE. DO YOU HAVE A PREFERENCE?
IT HAS TO BE STRETCHABLE FOR YOUR TRANSFORMA-TION....

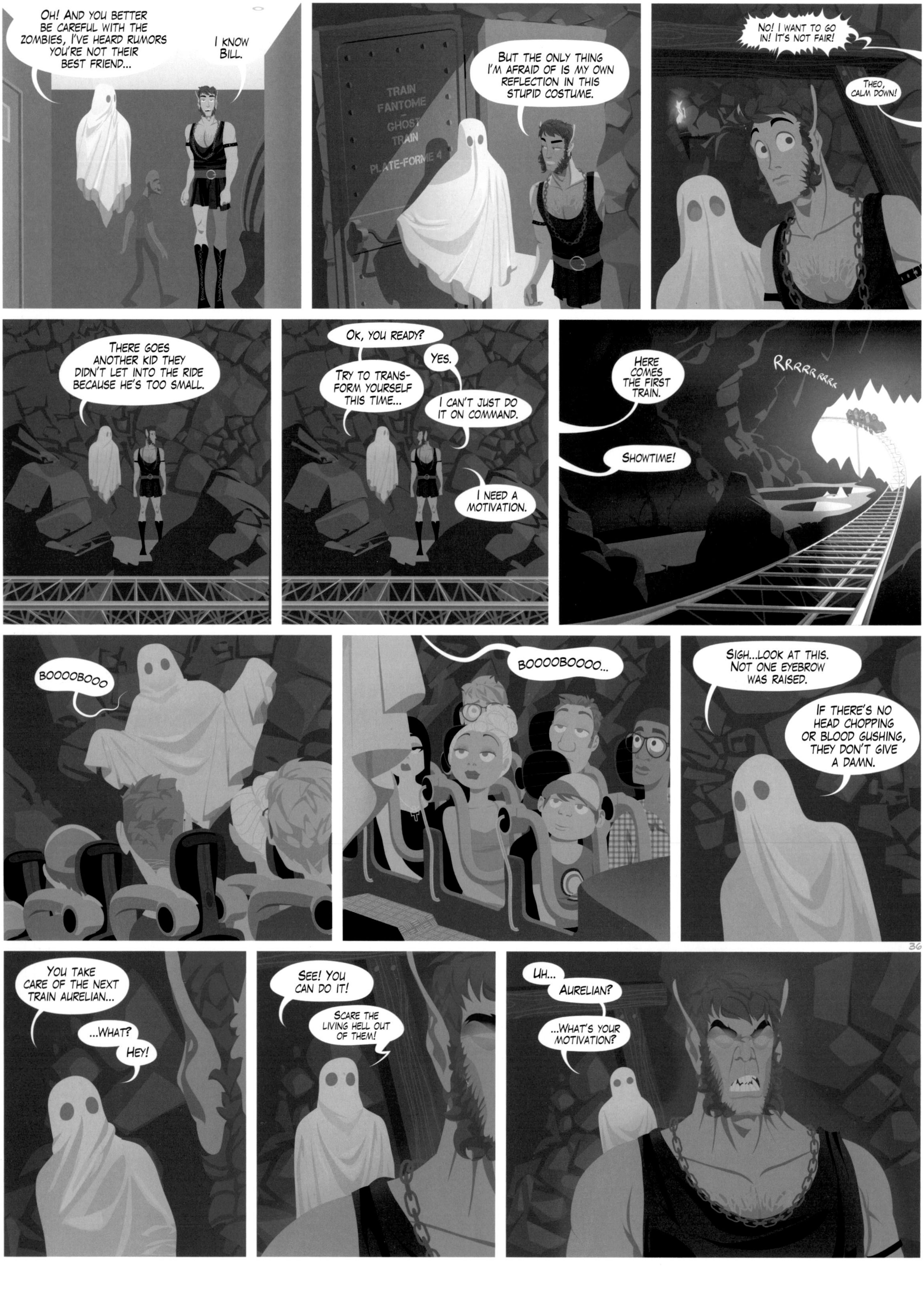

OH! AND YOU BETTER BE CAREFUL WITH THE ZOMBIES, I'VE HEARD RUMORS YOU'RE NOT THEIR BEST FRIEND...
I KNOW BILL.
TRAIN FANTOME - GHOST TRAIN
PLATE-FORME 4
BUT THE ONLY THING I'M AFRAID OF IS MY OWN REFLECTION IN THIS STUPID COSTUME.
NO! I WANT TO GO IN! IT'S NOT FAIR!
THEO, CALM DOWN!
THERE GOES ANOTHER KID THEY DIDN'T LET INTO THE RIDE BECAUSE HE'S TOO SMALL.
OK, YOU READY?
YES.
TRY TO TRANS-FORM YOURSELF THIS TIME...
I CAN'T JUST DO IT ON COMMAND.
I NEED A MOTIVATION.
HERE COMES THE FIRST TRAIN.
RRRRRRRRR
SHOWTIME!
BOOOOBOOO
BOOOOBOOOO...
SIGH...LOOK AT THIS. NOT ONE EYEBROW WAS RAISED.
IF THERE'S NO HEAD CHOPPING OR BLOOD GUSHING, THEY DON'T GIVE A DAMN.
YOU TAKE CARE OF THE NEXT TRAIN AURELIAN...
...WHAT?
HEY!
SEE! YOU CAN DO IT!
SCARE THE LIVING HELL OUT OF THEM!
UH...
AURELIAN?
...WHAT'S YOUR MOTIVATION?

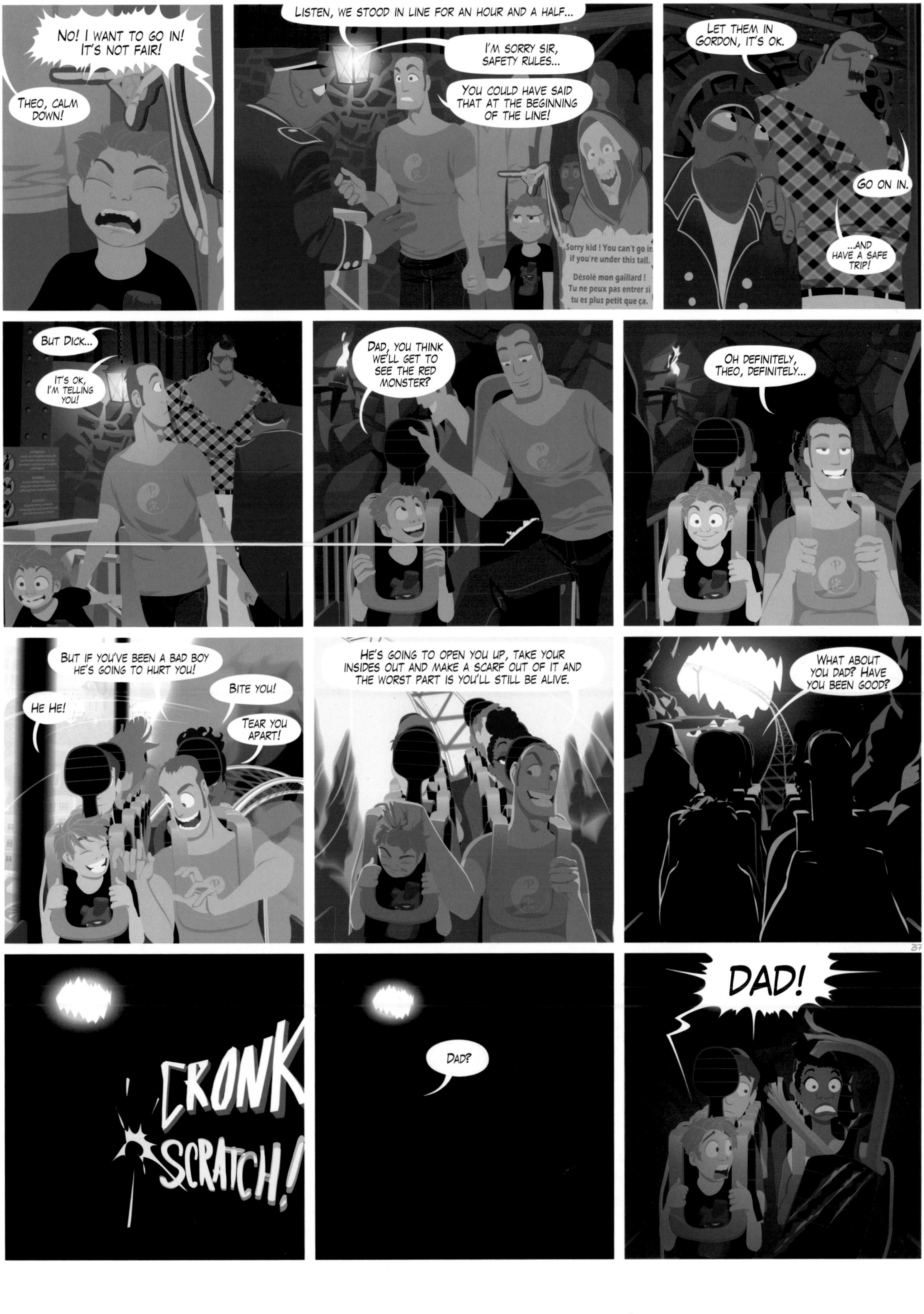
No! I want to go in! It's not fair!
Theo, calm down!
Listen, we stood in line for an hour and a half...
I'm sorry sir, safety rules...
You could have said that at the beginning of the line!
Sorry kid ! You can't go in if you're under this tall.
Désolé mon gaillard ! Tu ne peux pas entrer si tu es plus petit que ça.
Let them in Gordon, it's ok.
Go on in.
...and have a safe trip!
But Dick...
It's ok, I'm telling you!
Dad, you think we'll get to see the red monster?
Oh definitely, Theo, definitely...
But if you've been a bad boy he's going to hurt you!
He He!
Bite you!
Tear you apart!
He's going to open you up, take your insides out and make a scarf out of it and the worst part is you'll still be alive.
What about you dad? Have you been good?
CRONK
SCRATCH!
Dad?
DAD!

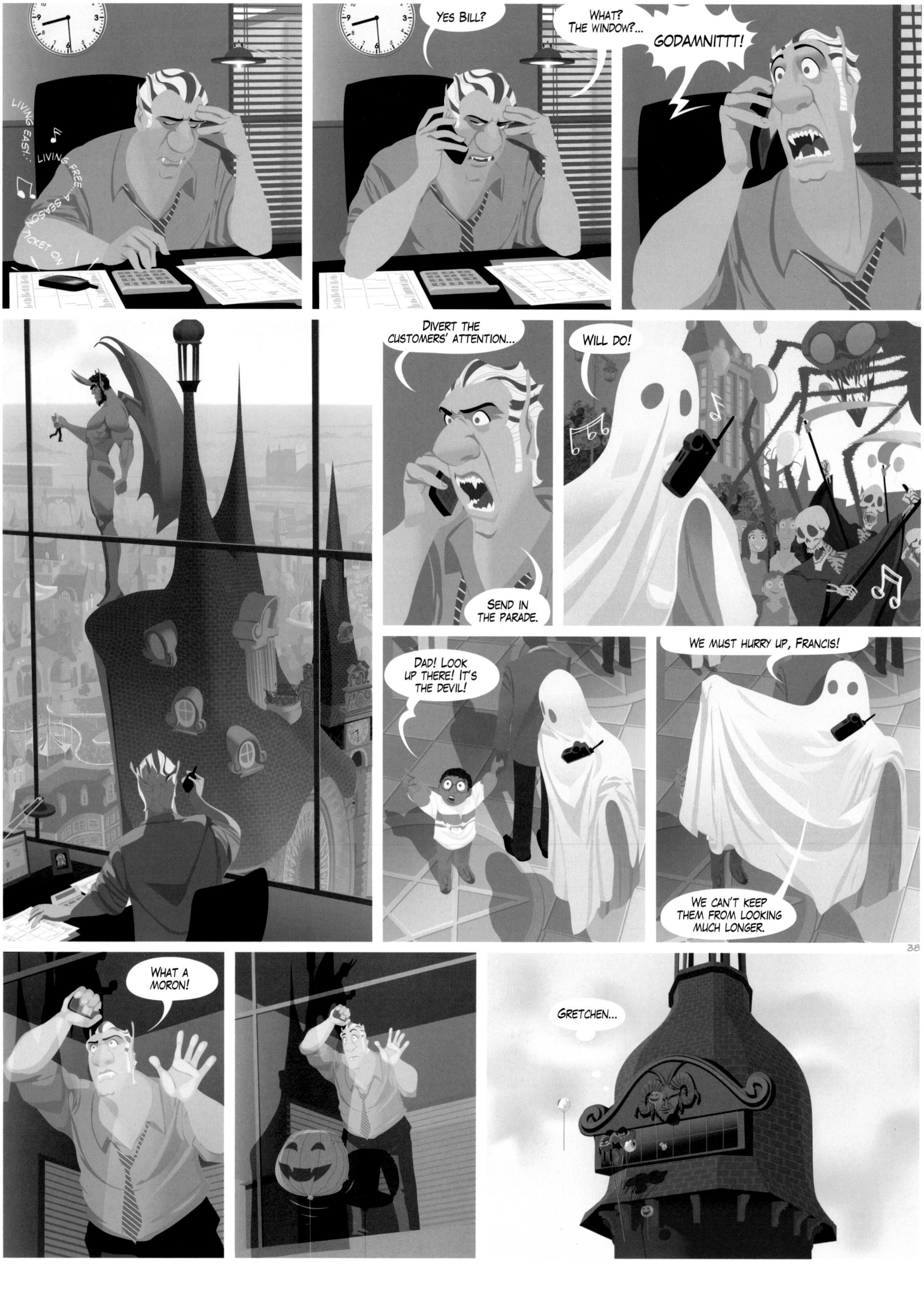
LIVING EASY... LIVING FREE... A SEASON TICKET ON
YES BILL?
WHAT? THE WINDOW?...
GODAMNITTT!
DIVERT THE CUSTOMERS' ATTENTION...
SEND IN THE PARADE.
WILL DO!
DAD! LOOK UP THERE! IT'S THE DEVIL!
WE MUST HURRY UP, FRANCIS!
WE CAN'T KEEP THEM FROM LOOKING MUCH LONGER.
WHAT A MORON!
GRETCHEN...

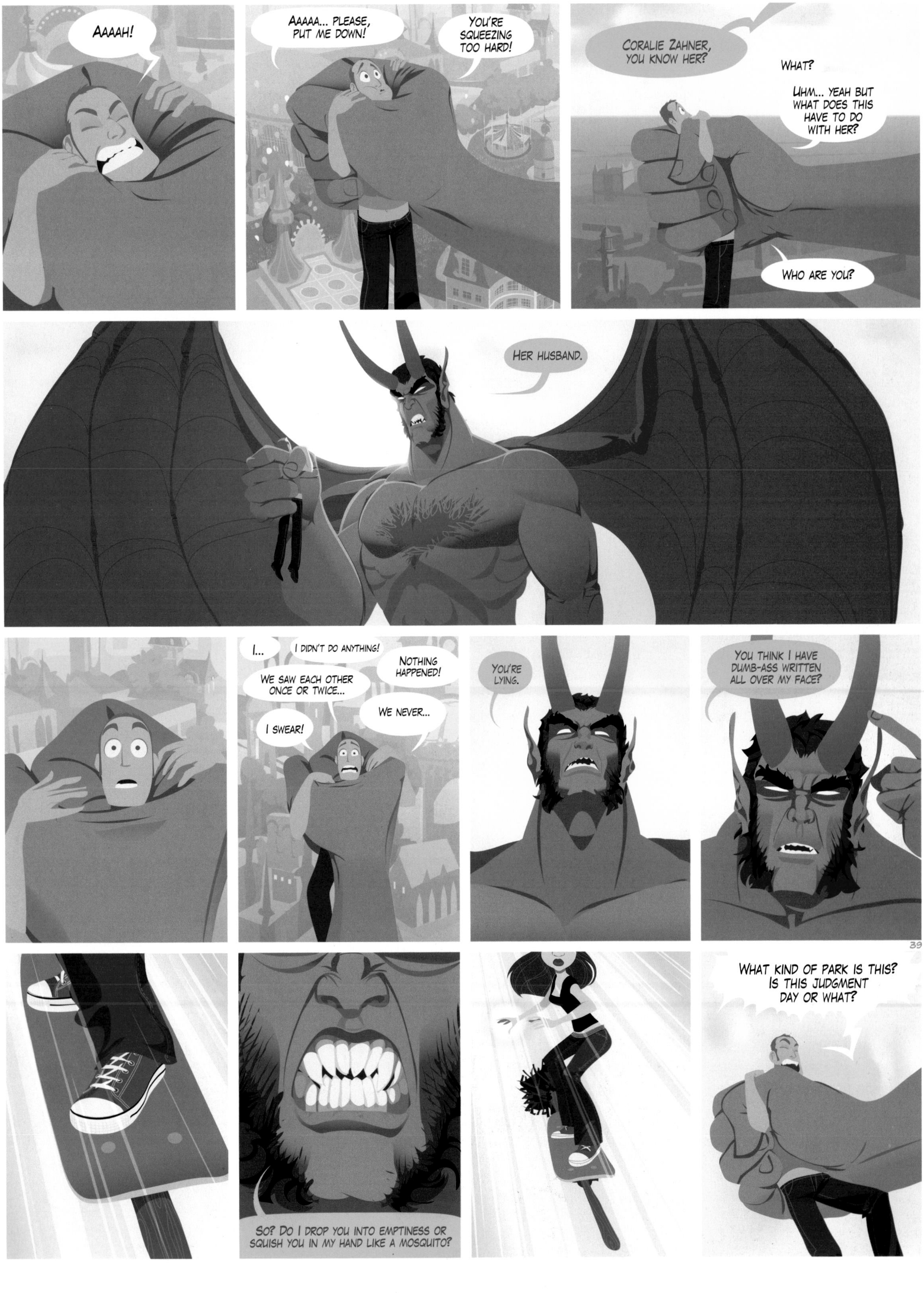
AAAAH!
AAAAA... PLEASE, PUT ME DOWN!
YOU'RE SQUEEZING TOO HARD!
CORALIE ZAHNER, YOU KNOW HER?
WHAT?
UHM... YEAH BUT WHAT DOES THIS HAVE TO DO WITH HER?
WHO ARE YOU?
HER HUSBAND.
I...
I DIDN'T DO ANYTHING!
NOTHING HAPPENED!
WE SAW EACH OTHER ONCE OR TWICE...
WE NEVER...
I SWEAR!
YOU'RE LYING.
YOU THINK I HAVE DUMB-ASS WRITTEN ALL OVER MY FACE?
SO? DO I DROP YOU INTO EMPTINESS OR SQUISH YOU IN MY HAND LIKE A MOSQUITO?
WHAT KIND OF PARK IS THIS? IS THIS JUDGMENT DAY OR WHAT?

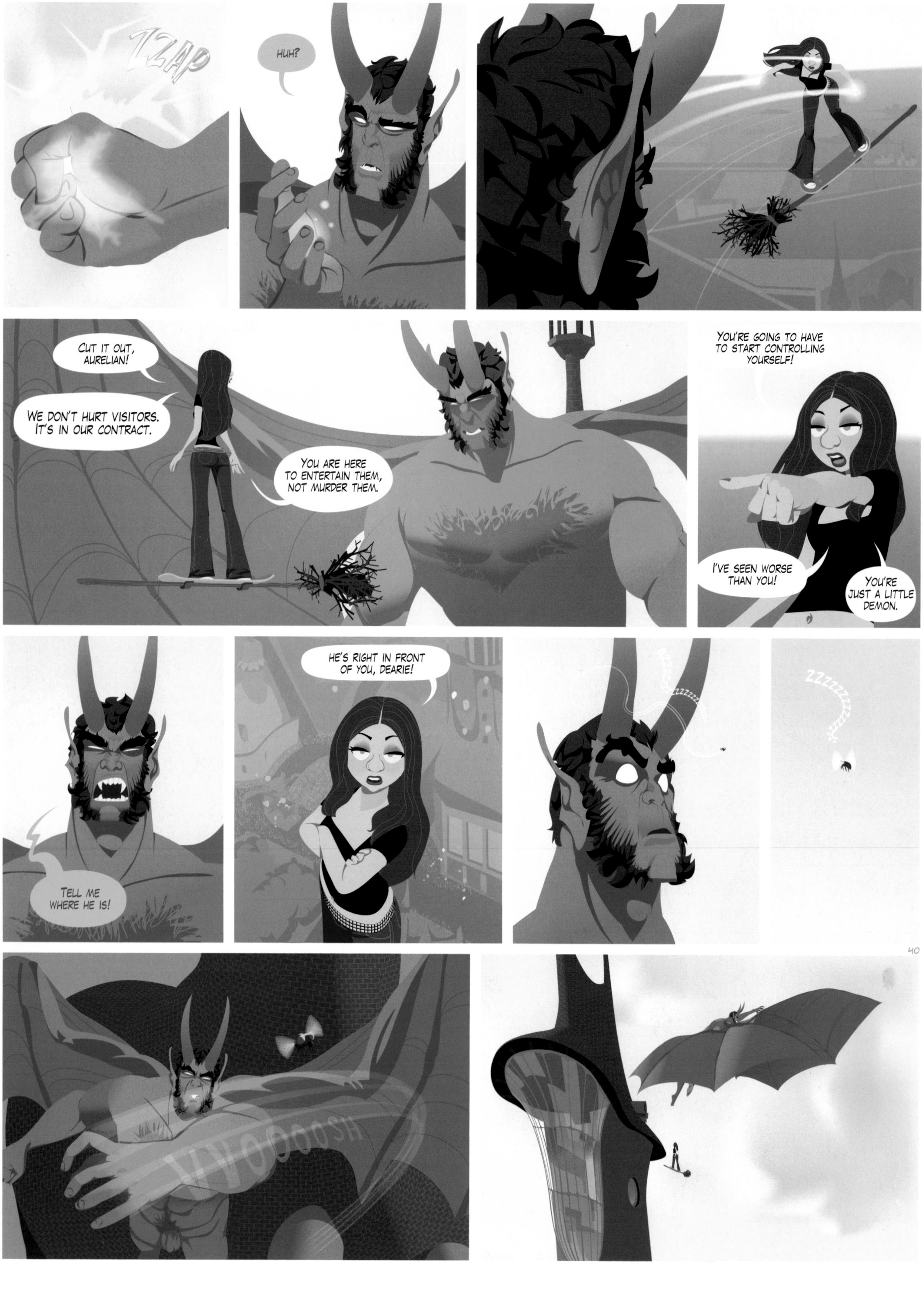
ZZAP
HUH?
CUT IT OUT, AURELIAN!
WE DON'T HURT VISITORS. IT'S IN OUR CONTRACT.
YOU ARE HERE TO ENTERTAIN THEM, NOT MURDER THEM.
YOU'RE GOING TO HAVE TO START CONTROLLING YOURSELF!
I'VE SEEN WORSE THAN YOU!
YOU'RE JUST A LITTLE DEMON.
TELL ME WHERE HE IS!
HE'S RIGHT IN FRONT OF YOU, DEARIE!
VVOOOOSH

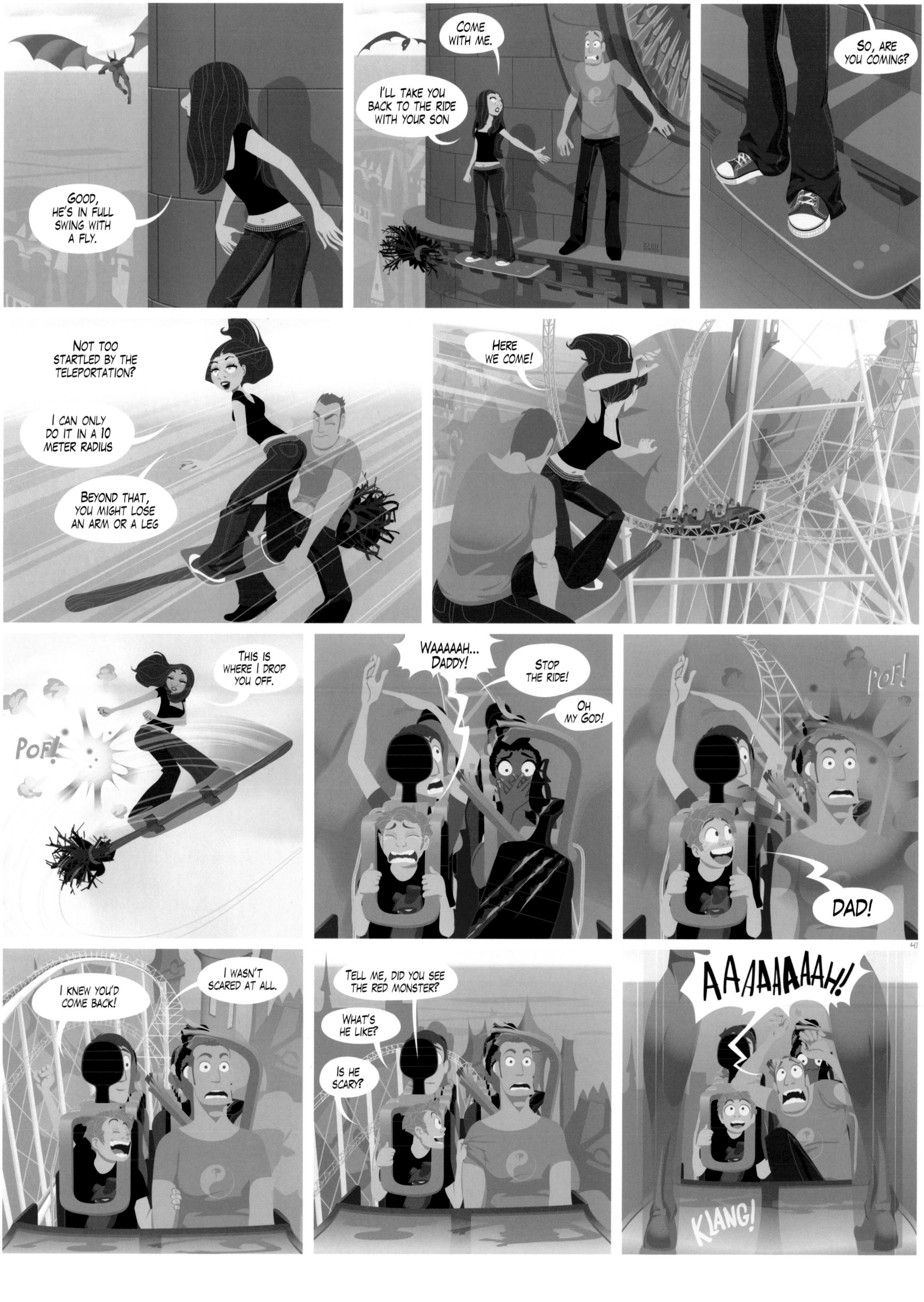
GOOD, HE'S IN FULL SWING WITH A FLY.
COME WITH ME.
I'LL TAKE YOU BACK TO THE RIDE WITH YOUR SON
SO, ARE YOU COMING?
NOT TOO STARTLED BY THE TELEPORTATION?
I CAN ONLY DO IT IN A 10 METER RADIUS
BEYOND THAT, YOU MIGHT LOSE AN ARM OR A LEG
HERE WE COME!
THIS IS WHERE I DROP YOU OFF.
POF!
WAAAAAH... DADDY!
STOP THE RIDE!
OH MY GOD!
POF!
DAD!
I KNEW YOU'D COME BACK!
I WASN'T SCARED AT ALL.
TELL ME, DID YOU SEE THE RED MONSTER?
WHAT'S HE LIKE?
IS HE SCARY?
AAAAAAAH!
KLANG!

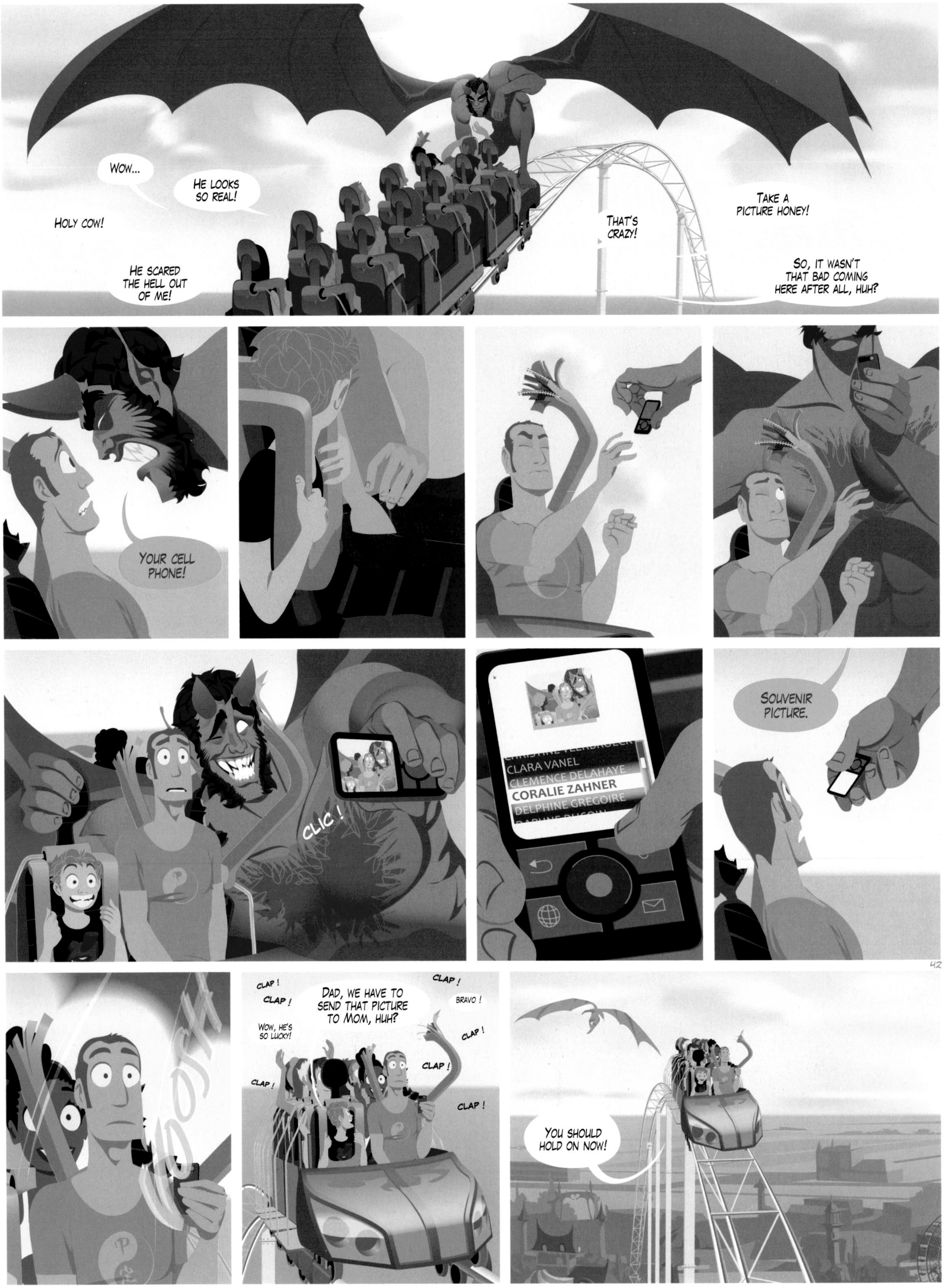
WOW...
HE LOOKS SO REAL!
HOLY COW!
HE SCARED THE HELL OUT OF ME!
THAT'S CRAZY!
TAKE A PICTURE HONEY!
SO, IT WASN'T THAT BAD COMING HERE AFTER ALL, HUH?
YOUR CELL PHONE!
CLIC !
CLARA VANEL
CLEMENCE DELAHAYE
CORALIE ZAHNER
DELPHINE GREGOIRE
SOUVENIR PICTURE.
CLAP !
CLAP !
DAD, WE HAVE TO SEND THAT PICTURE TO MOM, HUH?
CLAP !
BRAVO !
WOW, HE'S SO LUCKY!
CLAP !
CLAP !
CLAP !
CLAP !
YOU SHOULD HOLD ON NOW!

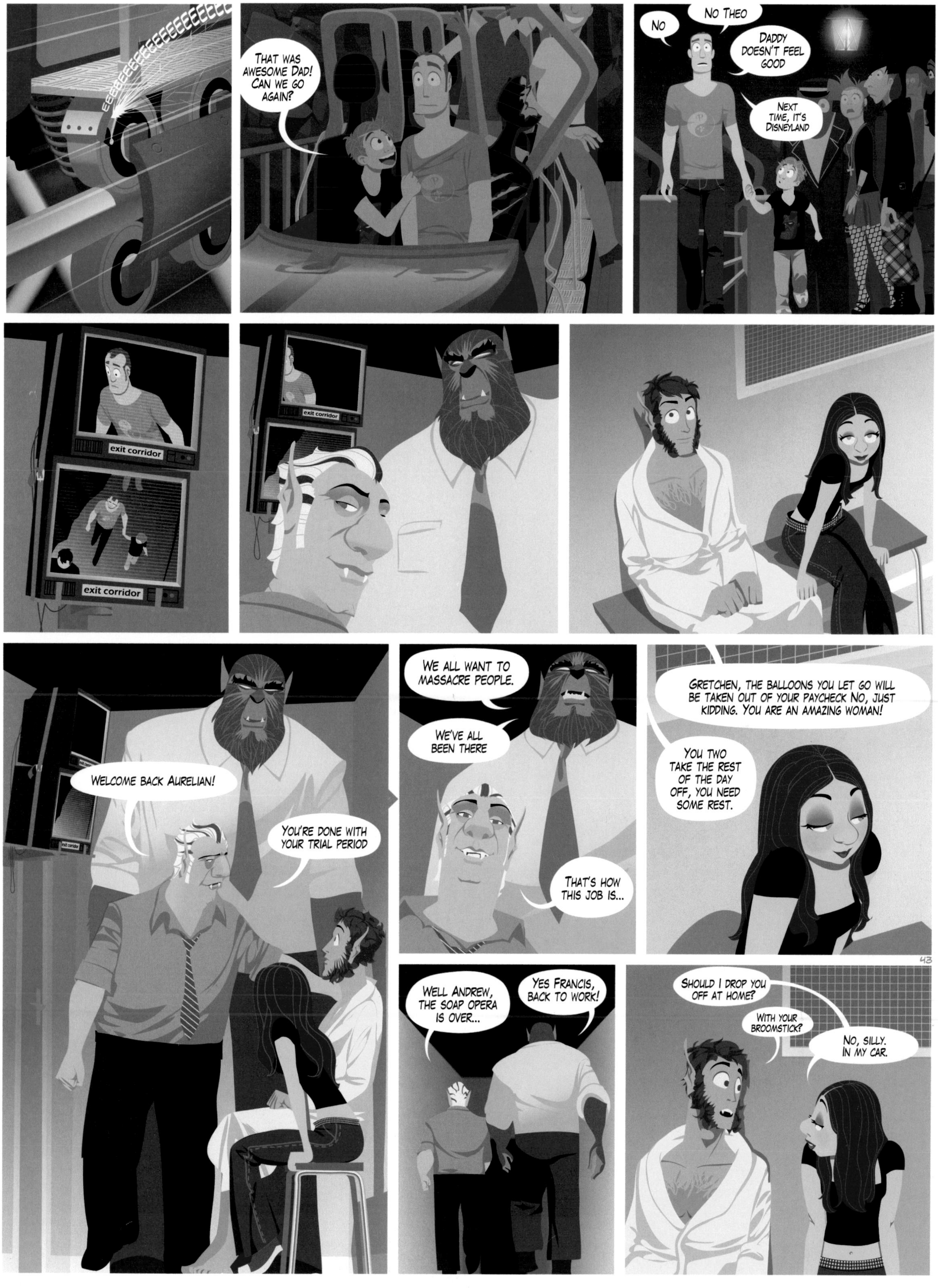
EEEEEEEEEEEEEEEEEE
That was awesome Dad! Can we go again?
No
No Theo
Daddy doesn't feel good
Next time, it's Disneyland
exit corridor
exit corridor
exit corridor
Welcome back Aurelian!
You're done with your trial period
We all want to massacre people.
We've all been there
That's how this job is...
Gretchen, the balloons you let go will be taken out of your paycheck No, just kidding. You are an amazing woman!
You two take the rest of the day off, you need some rest.
Well Andrew, the soap opera is over...
Yes Francis, back to work!
Should I drop you off at home?
With your broomstick?
No, silly. In my car.

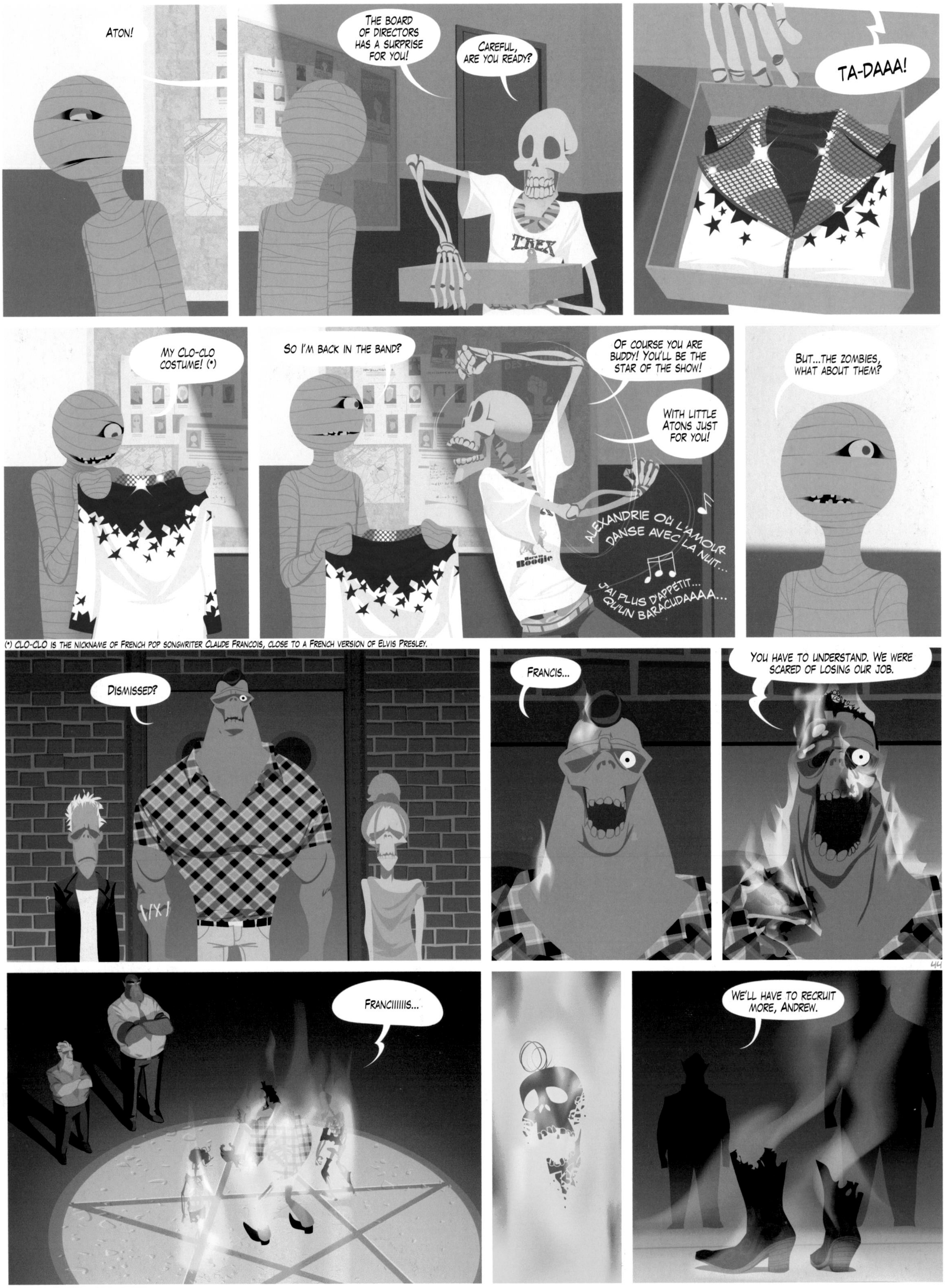
Aton!
The board of directors has a surprise for you!
Careful, are you ready?
T.REX
Ta-daaa!
My Clo-clo costume! (*)
So I'm back in the band?
Of course you are buddy! You'll be the star of the show!
With little Atons just for you!
Alexandrie où l'amour danse avec la nuit...
J'ai plus d'appétit... qu'un baracudaaaa...
But...the zombies, what about them?
(*) Clo-clo is the nickname of French pop songwriter Claude Francois, close to a French version of Elvis Presley.
Dismissed?
Francis...
You have to understand. We were scared of losing our job.
Franciiiiiis...
We'll have to recruit more, Andrew.

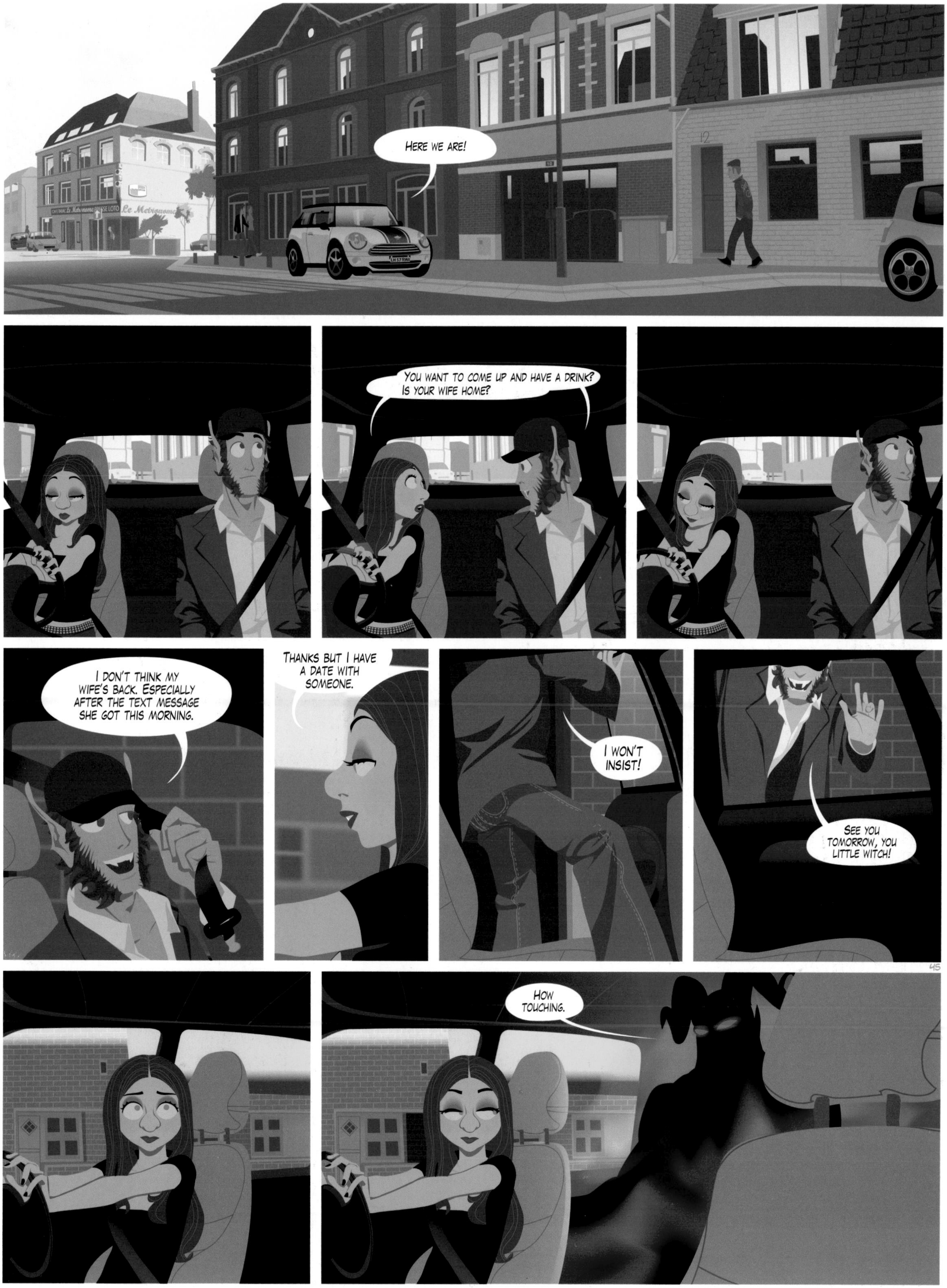
Here we are!
You want to come up and have a drink? Is your wife home?
I don't think my wife's back. Especially after the text message she got this morning.
Thanks but I have a date with someone.
I won't insist!
See you tomorrow, you little witch!
How touching.

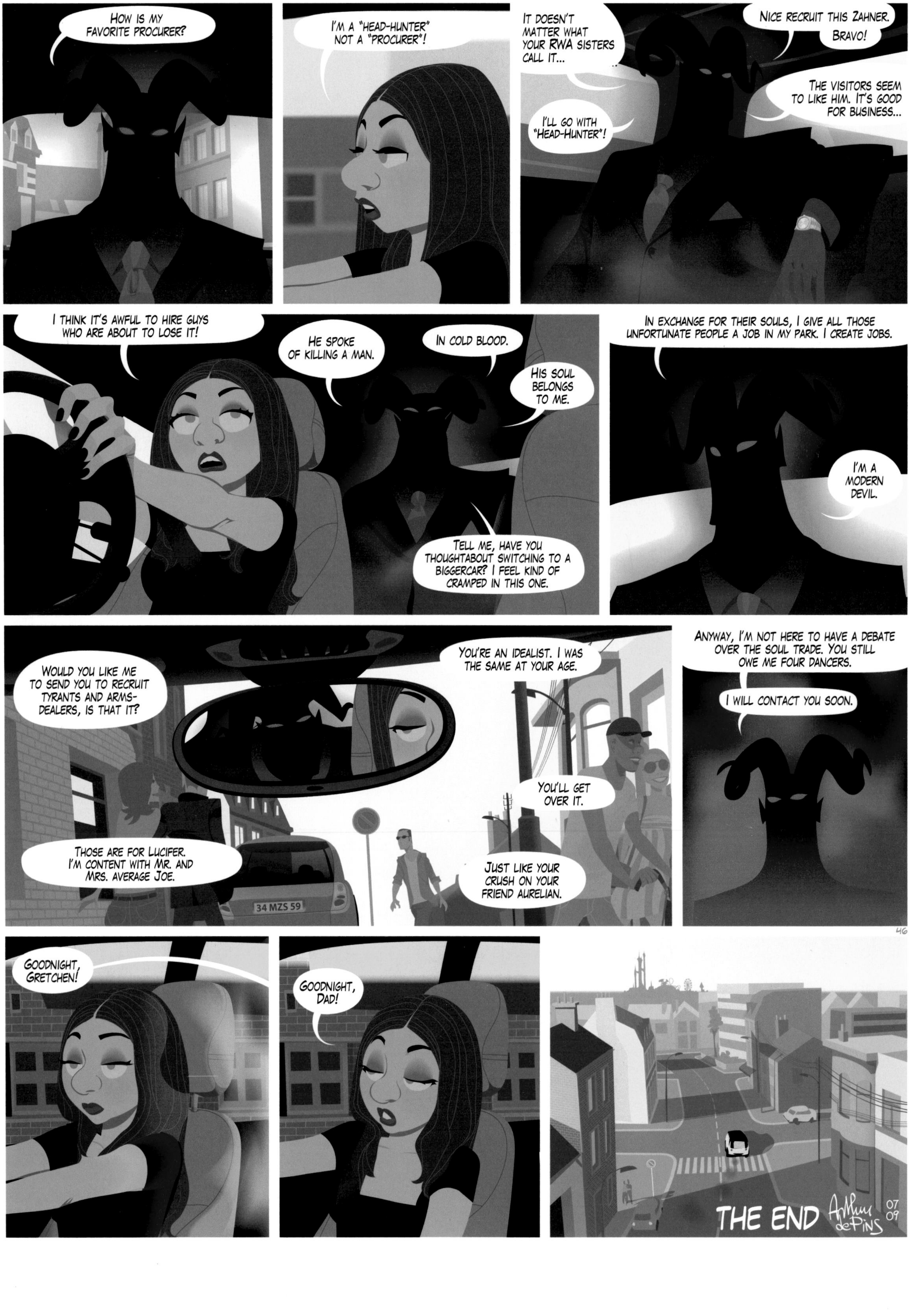
How is my favorite procurer?
I'm a "head-hunter" not a "procurer"!
It doesn't matter what your RWA sisters call it...
Nice recruit this Zahner.
Bravo!
I'll go with "Head-Hunter"!
The visitors seem to like him. It's good for business...
I think it's awful to hire guys who are about to lose it!
He spoke of killing a man.
In cold blood.
His soul belongs to me.
Tell me, have you thoughtabout switching to a biggercar? I feel kind of cramped in this one.
In exchange for their souls, I give all those unfortunate people a job in my park. I create jobs.
I'm a modern devil.
Would you like me to send you to recruit tyrants and arms-dealers, is that it?
You're an idealist. I was the same at your age.
34 MZS 59
You'll get over it.
Those are for Lucifer. I'm content with Mr. and Mrs. average Joe.
Just like your crush on your friend Aurelian.
Anyway, I'm not here to have a debate over the soul trade. You still owe me four dancers.
I will contact you soon.
Goodnight, Gretchen!
Goodnight, Dad!
THE END
Arthur dePins 07 09